T0113405

How to Hide Money from

Your Husband...and Other

Time-Honored Ways to

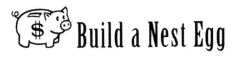 # Build a Nest Egg

The Best-Kept Secret of a Good Marriage

HEIDI EVANS

SIMON & SCHUSTER

Simon & Schuster
Rockefeller Center
1230 Avenue of the Americas
New York, NY 10020

Simon & Schuster and colophon are registered trademarks
of Simon & Schuster, Inc.

Designed by Ruth Lee

Manufactured in the United States of America

10 9 8 7 6 5 4

Library of Congress Cataloging-In-Publication Data
Evans, Heidi, date.
     How to hide money from you husband : and
    other time-honored ways to build a next egg : the
    best-kept secret of a good marriage / Heidi
Evans.
        p.   cm.
    1. Wives—Finance, Personal.   2. Marriage.
       I. Title.
       HG179.H878   1999
       332.024'0655—dc21   99-33635
                         CIP

ISBN: 978-0-7432-4249-3

For information regarding the special discounts for bulk purchases, please contact Simon &
Schuster Special Sales at 1-800-456-6798 or business@simonandschuster.com

Acknowledgments

Thank you, thank you, thank you, to:

Cynthia Crossen, the terrific *Wall Street Journal* editor who gave the green light to the original newspaper story I wrote on married women hiding money, an article that serendipitously became the seed for this book; the Media Studies Center in New York City for a four-month fellowship and the exquisite resources that launched the early reporting of the book, including researcher Lisa Meyer; John Goldman, New York Bureau Chief of the *Los Angeles Times*, who gave me a home in which to write and complete this project; Pam Forrester, babysitter extraordinaire and friend, who has made the writing life possible; Gail and Dan Collins, generous and special friends; Jane Dystel, ace literary agent and advocate; and my two superb editors at Simon & Schuster—Susan Arellano and Constance Herndon. I am also grateful to the following people for their insights and generosity: Kerry Brock, Ann Diamond, Myrna Felder, Richard Friedman, Ellen Miller Getlin, my funny neighbors Marion and Todd Godwin, Olivia Goldsmith, Felicity Nitz, Margo Howard, Bridget Macaskill, Don Pasinkoff, Charles Salzberg, Cassie Siefert, Barbara Sorid, Penny Stamler, and Sharyn Wolf. Special thanks to Judy Sheindlin, a warm and wise friend who met me on a moment's notice in a Second Avenue coffeeshop three years ago to help me shape my vision for this book; and to Josh Getlin—my husband, "in-house" editor, and best friend—a man who has given me everything for fifteen great years, including his paycheck. And lastly to the hundreds of women, named and unnamed, strangers and friends, who so generously opened their lives to me and now to all of you.

To the memory of my mother, Sara,
whose wisdom, wit, and love are part of all I do . . .

And to my wondrous little daughter, Alex,
who lights the path ahead.

Like mother, like daughter, like granddaughter . . .
and on it goes.

Contents

Foreword

By Judge Judy Sheindlin

The most important words for any woman to remember in her marriage and in life are these: In order to be happy, stress-free, and have the widest possible options, you must be financially independent.

Once you are dependent on anyone, your life options shrink and very often you are stuck in an untenable situation—whether it be a relationship, a marriage, a job, or anything else. And money is often the only ticket out.

Men are different. If a relationship ends, they can go out and support themselves much more easily than women can. They can dig ditches for $25 an hour. They can shovel garbage onto a truck. They have a great many roads open to them to earn a living. But women lack the brawn; they can't go out and do a construction job and comfortably deal with a heavy hydraulic machine for $30 an hour. They need to think ahead—and that's the central message of this book.

I've always tried to impress this upon my own daughters: The only way to true independence for a woman is to have a profession, a vocation, to at least have some money socked away for yourself—to cope with any kind of emergency. We all know life is full of emergencies. If you are being brutalized physically or emotionally, you need a financial escape hatch to take care of yourself. If a mate suddenly dies or disappears, you can't be left in the lurch, unprotected and bankrupt. Think of it as insurance. You don't anticipate that there is going to be a flood or a tornado suddenly destroying your home and driving you out of it. But you certainly prepare for it by taking out home owner's or flood insurance. The odds of dropping dead at forty-five of a heart attack or cancer are slim, yet we all buy medical and life insurance. *Having your own money is marriage insurance,* short and simple!

Yet women rarely have such wisdom or foresight when it comes to their relationships. Look at the divorce statistics in this country: We know that nearly half of all marriages in the United States fail. And this means, among other things, that if you spend $50,000 on a wedding, there's a good chance it's money down the drain. Think of it—that fifty-fifty shot is a much higher percentage of risk than that of dying from a heart attack or a stroke or cancer. It's much higher than the chances of being driven out of your home by a fire or a flood. But we don't prepare for these eventualities in our lives, in our fundamental relationships. And women can pay a huge price for this.

That's why we have to take action, starting at an early age, to squirrel away the money we all need to handle life in all its twists and turns. Unless we have millions socked away in a trust fund—and most of us don't—women need to give themselves a measure of financial independence, something totally separate from the men in their lives. Take it from someone who knows.

I had two small children when my first marriage ended in divorce. Yes, it was a draining experience for our family, but I had a law degree. I never felt frightened that I would not be able to support myself and my kids. I didn't have much money in the bank—which was a mistake—but at least I had a degree, a way to earn a living. And that's important for any working woman.

For millions of women who don't work outside the home, the lesson is no less important. However you do it—whether you hide money secretly or build a financial nest egg with your husband's full approval—you need to plan for the future and create that security. The older you get, the more important it becomes.

It's not just a lesson for the rich.

We've all known people in low- and middle-income homes where the husband comes home from work and turns over his paycheck to his wife. She pays all the bills; she gives him a weekly allowance. He doesn't want to know about money, and on the surface it looks like she's in control.

But what if that marriage breaks up tomorrow? He still has his job, but she has nothing. Any idea that she was "controlling" her financial future is gone. So the financial message for *all* women could not be more simple: Be smart. Never feel trapped. Do what needs to be done.

Believe me, I've done this in my own home for years. And it's not just because I'm planning for an uncertain future, or that I don't trust or love my husband. I do this as much *for* him as for me. By putting away money, I have the freedom to do many things, like buy him an extravagant birthday present or get something for one of our five kids that's very expensive. This kind of money doesn't grow on trees, but because I've been saving religiously— for myself—the money is there when we need it. I also do this because my husband, God bless him, is one of the world's great spenders. He buys things that please him, makes big purchases on a whim, and he doesn't worry about the future.

I worry about the future. A lot.

He may get angry with me sometimes and say: "Don't tell me what to do with my money." So the answer is simple. I have built up my own nest egg, I have my own accounts. And that, frankly, is where our family's financial protection comes from. Somebody has to do it—*and women must do it because they are more vulnerable to life's vagaries.* Unfortunately, millions don't have a clue—and that's why a book like this is so important for your overall health and well-being.

Having your own money also becomes urgent when your marriage or relationship doesn't work out. If it comes to pass that my present marriage should end—or if I pass away before my husband—I still want control over the money and security I have built up. *Nothing* would tick me off more than another woman—and that includes a subsequent Mrs. Sheindlin, thank you very much—ending up with 25 cents of my hard-earned money. I don't want her to get her hands on a penny, not on $100,000, not on anything. I would turn over in my grave if any person other than my husband or the children or our grandchildren ended up with that money. So I must do whatever is necessary to protect this money. No one outside my family is going to get that cash. I'd rather put it in a box and carry it with me down into the grave taped to my tush!

Ladies—protect what you have, now and in the future! You have to learn about the big bad world of finance, understand how wills, trust funds, and stock markets operate. More than ever before, you need to grow up and start playing the same financial angles that men have been playing for years.

I've seen a lot of their games, believe me. As a family court judge in Manhattan for fifteen years and now as television's Judge Judy, there's very little that has escaped me in the way of financial chicanery and the hell that couples go through over money. And what I have seen most commonly is truly depressing: Women are not prepared for the sudden end of their marriages or relationships, especially when it comes to money. In far too many cases of domestic abuse, women are reluctant to leave, mainly because they have no idea how they will support themselves without a man in their lives. They are powerless on perhaps the single most important issue facing them and their children.

I speak about this when I address groups around the country. I recently gave a talk in Nevada to professional women and told the audience that the greatest single favor they could do for their daughters—and their sons—would be to imbue them with the gift of financial independence, to give them the wisdom to understand the value of money at an early age and to plan their lives accordingly.

This goes double for women because they are not merely being independent for themselves; usually there's a family involved. They should *never* feel guilty about squirreling away enough money to take care of themselves and their children. They should never feel as if they are cheating if they have the wherewithal to stand on their own. That's true if a woman is forced to bail out of a lousy first marriage, or if she is worried about taking care of her children in an uncertain second marriage, or if a husband suddenly dies or is incapacitated and the wife has to be the single provider for the family.

Smart women have been taking care of business for decades.

My father was a dentist, but my mother took care of the money. He totally absolved himself of any financial responsibility, because his two hands were in someone else's mouth much of the time. If she went out for an hour or two, she would quite literally go through his pants pockets—while he was wearing them—to make sure he didn't take in any additional cash while she was out to lunch! She'd just dip into his pockets with one smooth movement, taking out whatever was there. My mother treated his money like her money, and also kept a little nest egg of her own.

I've learned these lessons in my own life. Today, I don't have a little hiding place at home where I stash money. I have a Merrill Lynch money market account. It's my personal checking account—my personal financial independence. My husband knows about it, but even if he didn't, or opposed the idea, I would take that money and

16

keep it separate. Every woman should do the same.

We're not just talking about six-figure, high-interest accounts. Let's talk small. Women should start reading this book, and saving money, in their twenties. It's easy to get started: You just take a dollar out of your wallet, every day, and put it in a jar. What do you spend a dollar on that's so important? Two packs of Life Savers or gum, if that. Ladies, take that same dollar and sock it away. At the end of the month, take it out of the jar and put it in a savings account. At the end of five years, by the time you are twenty-five to thirty, with interest and the money compounded, you could have as much as $2,000 saved up.

That money could turn into a small fortune if you do this faithfully throughout your life. You'll reach a point when you're thirty and say: "A dollar a day? That's ridiculous. I'm going to take out five dollars a day—or ten." If you keep doing this, by the time you're fifty the money you have on hand—separate from everything else you've saved—could be astronomical! It's the key to independence that every woman needs, and it starts with one dollar.

Today, young people think they're financially invincible. They think they'll always be able to earn a living somehow, and some may be right. But for any woman to think this way is absurd. If you're earning $200 a week, you can still take money and sock it away. Whether you have job security or not, the relationships you're going to encounter in life are not permanent. There's no guarantee that any man will be around forever. So get smart!

Remember, marriage is not a dress rehearsal for something else. If you become miserable in that relationship, you either will or will not have the financial means to get out of it. You have to be able to say good-bye when the time comes—or pay a terrible price for the rest of your life.

If you have a happy marriage, all the more reason to build a nest egg that can make a huge difference for both of you and your children. He may raise his eyebrows when he learns that you've been stashing cash—but how angry will he be when you pay for a vacation he thought was impossible, or if you can help pay for a college education that neither of you thought was in reach?

Men are funny creatures. Some will go ballistic if they learn you're taking care of your own needs. But others will react very differently. Some of the smarter men in our midst will say: "You know, it's true. That little bit of financial security is very important to her, and it makes her more of a partner!"

What it really comes down to is this: If your mate has confidence in you, he should *want* you to feel comfortable. If he wants you to feel secure and he has the strength of character to tell you this, it's all the more reason to be financially independent. Believe me, this kind of man won't be royally miffed if he discovers your secret account. If he's really Mr. Right, he'll laugh it off and say: "Yeah, well I guess if you have $5,000 stashed away, you have $10,000." That money simply means that you're more comfortable and more secure in your marriage. It makes you happy, so there's no downside.

However, if you have a mate who wants you to feel

dependent, no matter how much you argue to the contrary, it's all the more reason to build a financial future independent of him. If he insists on dominating you, you simply must empower yourself with an individual nest egg. It may not seem like a big deal when you're starting out, in your twenties, but it could become an impossible situation in your forties and fifties if you don't take these elementary steps.

This is a win-win situation, ladies. It's not simply a question of *if* you should do this. You *must* do this.

So ordered,
JUDGE JUDY

"It's a very sacred thing, the nest egg. . . . .The egg is a protector like a god, and we sit under the nest egg, and we are protected by it. Without it, no protection. Want me to go on? It pours rain. Hey, the rain drops on the egg and falls off the side. Without the egg, wet! It's over."

—*Albert Brooks in the film* Lost in America

Introduction

When all 105 pounds of my aunt Lee was carted out of her New York City apartment at the age of ninety-one, it came as no surprise to the women in our family that a bankbook with $50,000 was found buried in her top drawer.

"Remember to shove a little down south from what your husband gives you every week to run the house," she told my mother and all the other young married women in our family. "For a rainy day. For yourself, for the children. You never know when it will come in handy. Be smart."

The humble wife of a raincoat manufacturer had amassed her little fortune by stashing away a few dollars every week for sixty-five years, unbeknownst to my uncle Irving.

Her three sons—a dentist, a scientist, and a dog trainer—were dumbstruck when they discovered the bankbook.

"How the heck did Mom get her hands on this kind of cash?" exclaimed Seymour Evans, the Scarsdale dentist, shaking his head. Seymour's wife, Edith, who has been quietly following her mother-in-law's priceless advice for the last thirty-eight years, smiled knowingly to herself and said, "It beats the heck out of me, Sy."

Thus were born the Evans family's "Shove It Down South" accounts. Charles Schwab could do a lot worse.

You never forget such family stories—and Aunt Lee's eventually inspired an article I wrote for *The Wall Street Journal* about married women who hide money from their husbands. As I interviewed women around the country from all walks of life, I was amazed by how many of them, including the highly successful, said they kept a secret or separate stash. The amounts ranged from $300 to $200,000. The women ranged from a twenty-six-year-old lawyer to an eighty-three-year-old homemaker who had been hiding her money for forty years in a cigar box covered with scripture that she called her "Jesus box."

It quickly became obvious that this practice of having a nest egg of one's own was not confined to the Aunt Lees of this world—that is, struggling immigrant wives. Not by a long shot. This exists across cultures—Chinese women call it *hui*, Japanese women call it *tonomoshia*, Americans women call it a nest egg, Jewish women a *knipple*, and Caribbean women a *sous-sous*. As I spoke with working-class and professional women, stay-at-home moms and grandmothers, it became clear that I had tapped into a rich vein among women of every age and station. "Get real!" a secretary I met on the subway told me one night when I asked her if she saved money on the side. "Doesn't everybody?"

All of the women—and men—you will meet in this book are real. And so are their stories. Their names and some details have been changed only when it was necessary to protect their privacy, their children, or their nest eggs. Whether they earn $25,000 or $200,000, all women have certain common threads in their lives: concerns about financial security for themselves and their children; the desire to make some decisions independently of their husbands; questions of trust and the balance of power in their marriages. The more women I spoke to about this phenomenon, the more light it cast on a larger truth: Money is feminism's next frontier.

In the war between the sexes, money and what it represents unite women in a sisterhood that transcends politics, social status, and anything else. Money—not sex—is the key prize in the struggle between most couples. If you want to find the flash point of conflict and resentment in the lives of most American couples, the friction that dwarfs all others, follow the buck. The wallet is the window into the soul of marriage.

Today, believing that our men will always be there, that they will be loyal and loving until death or divorce do you part is right up there with "I'll respect you in the morning" and "My wife will never find out." With the divorce rate soaring and those adorable young interns showing no signs of going away (darn!) we'd be crazy not to cover our assets.

And for those who stay married, having such a stash may be the greatest gift of love you ever give your mate. What husband wouldn't be thrilled to have $100,000 appear out of nowhere? Just think of the possibilities, of what you could do with that wad of cash. You could buy retail, help your kids through college, or go on that much-dreamed-about second honeymoon.

Any woman who is tempted to put down this book and say "It's not for me" needs to read this book even more. We are not talking grand larceny—we're talking grand planning for the future. You should put money aside whether you love your husband more than life itself, or if you just tolerate him, or if you know deep down that you won't be sharing the same toothpaste forever.

So what are you waiting for?

1

Women, Their Men, and Their Money

Twenty Ways to Build Your Nest Egg

"Will he ever be able to produce revenue again?"

"If *anything ever happens to me,*" Sally confided to her sister, "there is $10,000 hidden in my black suede boots in the closet. He doesn't have a clue."

"He" is her husband, Jeff. She, like millions of American women, keeps a private nest egg. Her reason: Although Jeff has a lot of money, he doesn't like to spend it. And she must live with what he gives her.

Although Sally is raising their four young children and running a bustling household, Jeff, a movie executive, has convinced her that since *he* earns the money, *he* owns it. Many men have that view. Sally has no say in the big-money decisions—where they live, what kind of car they drive, or how they invest. She enjoys living well, not extravagantly. He can sleep on the same sheets he's had since college. Two different money personalities. She wishes he were different and that she could be his partner rather than his child. So she's been squirreling away $100 a month from the monthly household check he's given her for the last ten years.

"In case I get really fed up one day, at least I'll be able to pay for a lawyer," says Sally. "It's my security. He has a great salary. The kids are taken care of. But what do I have, really? I'm thirty-nine and I've been home raising our children for fifteen years. This just makes me feel better, having a little something of my own."

Although she bristles under their monetary arrangement, Sally has tried to keep her sense of humor. When El Niño's rain and mud slides were threatening to devastate the dry hills of southern California, the family evacuated their Malibu home and began to head south. As their station wagon nosed its way down the Pacific Coast Highway behind hundreds of other petrified evacuees, Sally suddenly remembered the money in her closet and made her husband turn back. "Oh my god," she blurted out, "I forgot the kids' birth certificates!" With darkened skies overhead, she ran back inside, dumped the crumpled $100 bills into a black overnight bag, and slept that night with her kids snuggled around her and her money safely tucked under her head.

A Nest Egg of Your Own

This elaborate dance between men and women has been going on since the beginning of time and, like an extramarital affair, it's almost never discussed. Until now.

Face facts, ladies. Virtually half of you will be divorced in your lifetime. Or, to be blunt, the half of you who say "I do" will one day say "I'm done!"

Are you financially prepared for what comes next? Do you have a dollar in the bank *just in case* . . .

He runs off with a sweet young thing who thinks JFK is an airport?

He drops dead and leaves you, the mortgage, the kids, and his aging parents in the lurch?

He suffers a midlife crisis and decides he'd rather spend his days hang gliding than putting in fourteen-hour days at his law firm?

Are you prepared?

Probably not.

And if you are among the lucky 50 percent who live happily ever after, do you have the kind of relationship in which you can buy yourself something, go somewhere, or give a gift to someone without having to "meet and confer" with your husband? Do you have money put away for those rainy—and expensive—days that drizzle into everyone's life? Like an unexpected medical crisis. Or you lose your job. Or there is a pair of $150 shoes you just have to have in every color.

Whatever your reasons—and everyone has them— you need money of your own. You may not buy this notion now, but by the time you finish this book, you'll be running to put your hands in his pants—or wherever he keeps his wallet.

Look, no one wants to be sneaky when they start out in a marriage. Of course it would be best to be forthright and say: "I am saving money for our security or my security just in case." But relationships with men are complex and often contradictory, and unfortunately not every woman is able to stand up and say she wants this safety net without paying some kind of price within the marriage.

So consider some of the cold, hard facts of women's lives:

- After divorce or separation—which affects 48 percent of all women—their income typically drops by more than one third.

- Women save only about half of what men do.
- Men still dominate the top jobs in the executive suites and in government. Of America's *Fortune* 500 companies, only two are led by women. And working women still do 87 percent of the shopping, 81 percent of the cooking, 78 percent of the cleaning, and 63 percent of the bill paying according to a 1993 study by the Family and Work Institute.
- Women outlive men by an average of seven years, yet they are less prepared for their financial futures than men despite their need for a larger nest egg.
- Women further cripple themselves by failing to save, invest, and plan for retirement.
- Women are still second-class citizens economically, earning 76 cents to men's $1.00. They lose ground to men in the workplace because they leave jobs to bear children or to care for ailing parents, and even if they stay on the job, they bump up against the glass ceiling.
- In 1991, a national survey examining the "second shift," meaning the hours of housework that are done after a person comes home from a regular job, found that women put in twenty-eight hours a week of housework compared to just seven hours put in by their husbands. This was a slight improvement over 1968, when women put in thirty-three hours of housework compared to only two hours put in by men (and you heard them complain about every minute of it). "There has been some improvement but women are still

doing virtually everything," observes Claudia Goldin, a Harvard economics professor who studies gender issues.

If all that wasn't stark enough, no matter how far the sexual revolution has propelled women forward, society still favors men in crucial aspects of life. Men get two or three shots at marriage; they can start over with younger wives and new children they don't have to take care of the second time around either. (This time they just pay for the nanny.) For our labor, we get wrinkled and eat bad hors d'oeuvres at menopause support groups. Men are free to climb the career ladder to bigger salaries, pensions, and stock options. Many of us interrupt or sacrifice our careers (i.e., our economic independence) for our children and our mates. In return, we have pitiful pensions, if any, and laughable social security checks. The only males who make goo-goo eyes at us are not even on solid foods yet.

One of the only ways out of this terrible bind—saving money—isn't always easy for women or for couples who are just making ends meet. Money is spent on living expenses; it gets sucked into the house, the kids. There is really nothing left for so many women, which is why they are the largest group living in poverty in America. They don't have anything in the pension or Social Security systems because they spent all their time, energy, and money raising a family. What happens to these women when they get divorced in their fifties is that they have no skills and no retirement money either! As Christopher Hayes of the National Center for Women and Retirement Research has put it, "There is no question in my mind that we are

well on our way in this country toward duplicating another generation of impoverished older women."

We're All in This Together

While the women's movement is plagued with deep divi-
sions, the issue of who handles the money in a marriage—
and how—is a question that unites millions of American
females. What emerges from their voices is an unspoken
sisterhood, linking women who work with those who stay
at home, those who are single with those who are married
with children, all sharing a conviction that spans an ideo-
logical spectrum from radical feminists to born-again
moms. Invariably, their reasons all boil down to the same
things: security, freedom, and financial independence.
Whatever their politics, American women face a common
vulnerability when it comes to their men and their money.
It is an awareness and a fear that is powerfully felt but not
often talked about.

"Having a nest egg is like having life insurance,"
Donna Hanover, TV newswoman and the wife of New
York City mayor Rudy Giuliani, once told me at a party.
"So many of my friends do this. Could *they* tell you sto-
ries!"

First, Second, or Third Wives—Take Heed

Olivia Goldsmith, author of the best-selling *The First Wives
Club* and herself a veteran of marriage and money wars,
put it this way during a recent chat we had over lunch.

"It's very bad for women *not* to have their own money. We all need some security. I feel like men have been stealing from us long enough! You've got to have your own money and be in control of it—and not just a little bit either.

"Furthermore, society is not equitable. There are a lot more poor women than men proportionately and women don't get many of the second and third chances that men do. Someone once said, 'A soldier has many summers, but a woman only one.' I know a lot of successful women and so many of us have the same nightmare—that we are going to wind up as bag ladies."

Goldsmith urges women to be up front with their husbands rather than secretly put money away. But, she concedes, not every woman can be that honest without her husband hitting the roof, or worse.

"I'm an up-front kind of person. But I understand there are a lot of women who would read that and say, 'Yeah, you try being up front with MY husband. He'd start divorce proceedings.' I've even heard women say, 'If he knew I had money he'd hit me.' If I had to choose between being honest with a man and having my own money, I would choose having my own money."

That's what many women have had to decide.

Why Hide?

What you are going to learn from this book is, first, why you must put money away; the many different and creative ways you can squirrel away cash; what to do if divorce is on your horizon (hide more!); what men are up to (they're already hiding from you!); and, finally, what to do with your money once you have a nest egg of your own (invest and squirrel away some more!).

These lessons, as you will see, apply whether you are young—in your twenties or thirties and just starting out in a marriage—or you are looking down the gun barrel of that first divorce in your forties; whether you are embarking on a second marriage in your fifties or trying to make it on your own; and whether you and your husband are still united in your sixties and seventies and beyond.

The fact is that men have always had the money and the power that comes with it. And they are not about to give up either anytime soon. Let's face it, most of us don't come home to a Prince "My Wallet Is Open" Charming who says, "Take my money, please." With almost every purchase comes a free argument. Some are small, such as "Get off the phone, you are running up the bill," to "What do we need a big house for? I love our one-bedroom apartment. We are all so cozy here—you, me, and the triplets!"

Do What You Have to Do!

To be sure, honesty is the best policy. If you can be up front with your husband about having money of your own, do it! You are entitled. It makes you feel secure for 101 different reasons. Explain that the money will be for both of you one day, and if tragedy or divorce strikes, at least you have some protection. Unfortunately, not every man and marriage can handle such independent thinking and banking. Money is threatening to a lot of men.

It is also something they feel they must hide or control in order to keep the upper hand. If you don't think men are pros at this game, check out this small but telling item from the *Los Angeles Weekly's* "County Labor Update" in October 1997:

The Association of Los Angeles Deputy Sheriffs "won for its members a 10% increase spread out over three years. Added to that was a . . . one-time $2,100 uniform bonus and a $1,000-per-year uniform allowance. Insiders contend this last [benefit's] special charm is that it doesn't go on the paycheck, and hence needn't come to the attention of the deputies' spouses."

Herbert Glass, a certified public accountant in the Midwest for more than thirty years, says that he has seen men try almost every trick in the book over the years to keep their wives in the dark. Some forge their wives' signatures on the joint tax return because they don't want them to see what they have, others set up offshore trusts in the Cayman Islands. Says Glass, "Believe me, when it comes to protecting their own interests, men take the cake. They can afford professional advice. They can hide a lot if they are so inclined."

Consequently, many women feel they have no alternative to being secretive, given recurring tensions with their husbands over routine money management.

Kathy, a Massachusetts English teacher, opened a secret joint account many years ago for her fifty-two-year-old friend Barbara. The reason? Barb's husband gambles and spends money on anything that isn't nailed down. The monthly statement for Barbara's secret account is mailed to Kathy's apartment in Cambridge. If there is tax to pay on the interest come April fifteenth, Barbara gives her the money in cash. This way there is absolutely no paper trail to Barbara's house or husband. The two women dip into the account once a year for their "girls only" weekend in New York.

"Barbara could put her hands on several thousand dollars if her children ever needed it, and Dave would never know how," says Kathy. "What other choice does she have? Her husband is just a loser on the money front."

WATCH OUT FOR THOSE SECOND MARRIAGES!

If you are remarried with kids and a member of one of today's blended families, money tensions are never far from the surface. The ex-wife wants more alimony or child support. Your new husband wants you to help finance his children's Ivy League educations and new sports cars. You need your own nest egg so that you can give your kids what you want and not have to ask anyone's permission. One typical argument in the blended family goes something like this:

Second Wife: I'm taking $1,000 out of the checking account to help Ben pay his rent.

Second Husband: You're doing *what*? No way; I've worked too hard for this money and I'd rather see my own kids use it.

Vicky is all too familiar with these conversations. This fifty-four-year-old nurse from the Soviet Union married the man who helped her when she first arrived in America. They both have children from their first marriages. Today, she puts in six days a week on her feet as a massage therapist.

41

But instead of pooling her earnings with Bill's, Vicky puts most of her money in a secret bank account with her twenty-year-old daughter, Natasha, a college junior. A blunt and cheerful woman despite the hard years in Russia, Vicky says she loves her second husband very much. But when you've lived under a dictatorship—either governmental or spousal—a woman's independence is more important than love. She is deliciously guilt-free about her nest egg.

"Even if you have the most wonderful husband in the world, you must always think about yourself and your kids first," says Vicky. "Bill would never give what I want to give to my kids. Let me put it this way: Second husbands are like having a bridge in your mouth. It's comfortable, it's good, but it's not like having your own teeth."

BETTER TO HAVE A HORRIBLE JOB THAN A HORRIBLE MAN—MONEY IS YOUR TICKET OUT

If you have a controlling or a cruel husband, it makes no difference whether you are rich or poor. It still feels the same—lousy. Donna struggled with an abusive husband as a teenage mother in rural North Carolina until she got a good-paying job on the assembly line at a Perdue chicken plant.

"Although that job nearly cost me my health, it was my ticket out," said Donna. "My daughters and I were free and happy once I had my own money to escape this abusive man. Better to have a horrible job than a horrible man."

NICE GUYS DON'T EXEMPT YOU
FROM THE NEST EGG RULE

Even in peaceful marriages in which money doesn't seem to be a major issue, or in which women have large enough salaries to support themselves, women want and should have their own money. Why? Ask Helen.

The savvy, forty-six-year-old president of an environmental clean-up company in Houston has a whopping $200,000 tucked away in a separate account. It's a must, she says. "If there is a death or a nasty divorce, or if they lose their job," she says, "women can find themselves in the most destitute of circumstances. I've seen that happen too many times!"

Her accountant husband, Gary, is aware of her nest egg but has no access to it, which occasionally "raises a little fur." When he does bring up the subject, Helen tries to reassure him that he has nothing to worry about. If he ever needed the money for an emergency, she tells him, she would be there for him. No question about it.

All this sound familiar? Well, it is. Marital therapists report that 80 percent of the couples who seek counseling have issues over money, not sex. Because money is not just money. It's power, freedom, independence, self-esteem, and, if you're lucky, a weekend in Cancun with the personal trainer of your dreams. This is scary stuff for men.

True, women have redefined their roles with men at home and at work. And they also want to make some of the family's financial decisions. Whether they're housewives, blue-collar workers, or executives; whether they're young or old, rich or poor—women want and need cash to call their own. Here are some examples of the lengths they've had to go to.

Who's in Charge Here?

Liz, a Manhattan homemaker and former buyer for Saks Fifth Avenue, has a truly ingenious way to get her hands on cash without her hubby knowing a thing. Her husband, Bob, a silver-haired CEO of a *Fortune* 500 company, is willing to pay his wife's credit card bills, she explains. But he keeps her on a short cash leash as a form of control.

Curled up on the couch in a pair of elegant silk slacks, Liz says adamantly, "I do and have done everything for this man. I've made a beautiful home, entertained his business associates, and given up my own career to raise our children and devote myself to him. Why should he control how much cash I have? It's humiliating after all these years, don't you think?"

Liz has always loved to shop. She has spent many an afternoon sauntering in and out of Madison Avenue stores. She charges all her merchandise—Hermes scarves, Chanel bags, gold-and-diamond earrings, and size-ten dresses. Once a month, she invites several of her less affluent friends—women who have to work for a living—to "shop" in her "private boutique," her bedroom. She sells everything she has bought on her credit cards to her friends for half price—provided they pay in cash. It's a good deal all around. Her friends get a bargain. She gets cash, which she stashes in a Swiss bank. Her husband is none the wiser.

MEN NEVER KNOW THE PRICE OF A NIGHTGOWN

Allison, a New York businesswoman, confesses that she keeps a slush fund for her sister who lives in Los Angeles. Her brother-in-law is an idiot when it comes to saving money for retirement, so she is doing it for her sister. "Every year I send her a $14 nightgown in a pretty color, which he thinks is very expensive. But my real gift is putting a few hundred dollars in a brokerage account I started for her several years ago. By the time she retires, she'll have a nice piece of change."

LET HIM WEAR THE PANTS AS LONG AS YOU CHECK HIS POCKETS—WASH 'N' FOLD THOSE $50s

Phyliss's husband may wear the pants in the family, but she's the one who washes them. It's a good move, and profitable. Roger owns a hair salon in New Jersey and runs his business on an all-cash basis. Most nights when he comes home there are plenty of crumpled $50s in the front pockets of his jeans. Phyliss is only too happy to do his laundry, always checking the pockets first. Before throwing his Levi's into the washing machine, she exchanges the crumpled $50s with a stash of crumpled $5s she keeps in her dresser just for these occasions. She keeps her private stash behind the broken air-conditioning unit in her apartment.

45

"I wised up seven years ago, after I got tired of arguing with Mr. Cheap about things we needed in the house and things for our teenage daughter. Roger, like his father, doesn't part with a dime." So, like her mother before her, Phyliss keeps a nest egg for all the things she and her daughter want but hubby refuses to pay for.

So how much has she squirreled away? "Enough!" says Phyliss, waving her hand to show off a small gold ring her husband recently paid for without feeling any pain.

What's a Girl to Do?

Now the question becomes what to do with the nest egg once you've accumulated a bunch. You can invest the money, give a loved one a gift, or spend some of it on your dream. Here are the stories of how women handle their money and their men—told in their own words.

ME BIG SPENDER—YOU JANE

Jane, a San Diego newspaper editor and the mother of two, has her nest egg in real estate. She adores her husband, Phil, and plans to be with him for the duration. But it's been clear since they first met twenty years ago that

Phil was a BIG spender. Jane, ever the prudent one with an eye toward the future and planning for catastrophe, knew she would have to take their money matters into her own hands if she and Phil were going to have a retirement, a summer house, money to send their kids to college, and money to travel.

This is how they started out:

"Once, when we were dating, we drove to Los Angeles for a weekend and were pulled over by the state police for speeding. The officer ran a check on Phil and told him he owed $1,500 in parking tickets. I was shocked he had let them build up so high!

"Soon after the ticket episode, a merchant in a little truck came up to our door and said: 'This check bounced and I've come to collect!' I was mortified. I told Phil I would only marry him if he agreed to two conditions:

1. He turn himself into the court immediately and pay the $1,500 in parking tickets.
2. That I handle our checking and savings accounts. I would give him what he feels he needs, without going overboard either.

"In our house, Phil is the spender. I'm the saver. He convinces me that we can go to France when we really can't. So I use real estate as a way to force savings. Let me explain. I put money from both his paycheck and mine into a savings account. When it gets big enough and I see Phil starting to drool over a $15,000 rug in Macy's or a new $40,000 BMW, I buy another piece of property. We recently bought a summer cabin in the country on three acres of land. We paid CASH, thanks to me. Same thing with the house we own in San Diego—we paid for a lot of it in cash. He can handle that. He would never sell the property—in fact, he couldn't without me—and so we don't keep very much in savings since, if it was there, Phil would spend it.

"I knew things went too far when, years back, Phil bought a $5,000 rug for our living room. It never occurred to him what a terrible idea it was to have a fancy rug when you have two boys under the age of five and a shedding dog who chews on furniture! I realized at that point that Phil did this because we had too much disposable income in our checking account. So I just doubled our mortgage payment. I always try to be one step ahead of him and his itchy hands. He likes to spend money on expensive wine, clothes, travel, and his computer stuff. I know it bothers him not to be able to spend freely, but I also know he appreciates that we have our money invested well: Our boys have a country house they can go to in the summer, we have a home to retire to, and the other rental property we bought generates enough money to create a decent college fund for the kids. We even went to France one (just one) summer.

"Although I'm the better money manager, and I'm stealing money away from his paycheck and mine to invest in our properties, I want Phil involved in our finances on some level so he can see and understand what's going on. It's his job to take the statements and balance the checkbook. But I have to admit I made him give me back that job a few times because he wasn't really appreciating what our money situation was. When I said we were short of money, he replied: 'You always say that!' "

Not all women are as self-assured as Jane, to be sure. Part of her confidence comes from the time in which she grew up—the 1960s and 1970s. But for many other women, especially those raised and married in an earlier era, the struggle for independence within a marriage is not addressed openly. It was impossible for many women who came of age in the 1940s and 1950s to speak out for themselves, let alone do combat with their husbands over one of the most thorny aspects of marriage.

TILL DEATH (AND DOLLARS) DO US PART— A FINAL GIFT

Jan was a warm, proud, and religious woman who endured the humiliation of a philandering and spendthrift husband through forty years of marriage. Since Peter was not terribly discreet about his lust for young secretaries—one even became pregnant and successfully sued him for child support—everyone in Jan's Minneapolis community came to learn of her troubles. What little privacy the sixty-two-year-old Sunday-school teacher enjoyed in the early years of their marriage was destroyed.

Then, last year, Jan suffered another devastating blow. She was diagnosed with pancreatic cancer and given six months to live. During one of the final days of her life, she pulled a battered green suitcase out from under her bed and handed it to Ellen, her girlfriend of fifty years.

"Here," Jan said in a soft but emphatic voice, "I want you to have this." To Ellen's astonishment, the vinyl suitcase was packed with $100,000 in small, crumpled bills— singles, fives, tens, twenties—that Jan had taken from Peter over thirty-five years. It had been her way of reclaiming some dignity and leverage in an all but shattered relationship, and at a time when divorce was unthinkable. Since Jan and Peter had no children, Jan gave this extraordinary gift to her devoted friend. Peter would have been shocked by his wife's secret.

Stashing Cash for Both of You

One of the biggest obstacles to overcome is the idea that you're saving money only for yourself. It's certainly true in extreme cases—as in he's running off with his secretary and you have to make sure you aren't left holding the empty bag. But millions of women do this to *strengthen* a good marriage as well.

Sharyn Wolf, author of *How to Stay Lovers for Life—Discover a Marriage Counselor's Tricks of the Trade* and a psychotherapist, says that every woman should be putting away money for the future. Wolf herself has a nest egg, and says her husband has learned not to challenge her about it. He may think she's crazy, Wolf concedes, but he also knows how important it is to her sense of self that she have her own money, and that the last thing on her mind is leaving him. On the contrary. She has been able to treat him to a trip to Italy and many other pleasures.

"I don't know the derivation of the word 'nest egg,' but

I do know it's about giving birth to something, taking care of something, not about depriving somebody," Wolf says. More important, she notes, "Women who are worried about keeping a secret should keep in mind that secrets are not necessarily bad. Putting money away can be a wonderful thing for a relationship. A woman just needs to decide what she wants and ask herself, 'What is this money for?' Is it to financially protect herself and her family, or is it to have a necessary escape from a bad and unhappy marriage? BOTH REASONS ARE VALID."

Men Have Feelings, Too

So how do men feel about all this? Not surprisingly, they have strong feelings. Some are crushed. Some are infuriated. Some are thrilled.

Bob, a pianist, said his marriage ended soon after he found out his wife had stashed away tens of thousands of dollars while they were trying to make ends meet.

"I was a struggling musician for so long. We went nowhere. We ate spaghetti every night, never went to a movie. When I discovered she had socked this money away, and we could have lived so much better and enjoyed ourselves, I was devastated. It turned out this was a family custom and she was doing exactly what her mother and grandmother told her to do." (Okay, so not every woman is perfect.)

Don, a retired schoolteacher who is married to another teacher twenty years younger, could barely contain his rage at just the thought that his wife could have secreted thousands away. In their seventeen years of marriage there has always been one communal pot of money. They shared their salaries, paid for everything together, and made joint decisions about how money was saved and spent. His income is now much smaller than hers and there is financial pressure on him to come up with enough money to find a home for his ninety-two-year-old mother.

"If my wife had done such a thing, it would be the greatest betrayal," said Don, his blood pressure rising as he spoke. "I have always assumed that we are both playing by the same rules we agreed on when we got married. I would be amazed, astounded, and not a happy camper. Money is a very delicate issue. I am a very generous person. Whatever is mine is yours. Whatever you want, you can have.

"That is the unwritten Eleventh Commandment. Thou shall not break the financial agreement. You do something like that, you'd better nail your socks down to the floor!

"On the other hand, if the guy is walking all over the gal, 'Please,' I would tell her, 'Steal everything!' I'd give a standing ovation to a woman who has hidden money away to escape an abusive man. But if everyone is playing by the rules, this is a serious no-no."

David, the headmaster of a New Jersey private school, says he tells his three daughters that it's important for them to be independent and not lean on a man. But he stops short of endorsing secret accounts, saying it could undermine a marriage before it starts. "Everything in our family is out in the open and shared," he said with the quiet confidence of a man who is at ease with himself and his wife of sixteen years, Leslie.

"Oh, really?" say the raised eyebrows on Leslie's lovely face as she pretends to ignore the conversation. She beckons me over to the porch of their Cape Cod summer cottage and confides, "I have $20,000 in stocks and bonds he doesn't know about."

When David found out, he was thrilled. "What a wonderful surprise! It makes me happy to know my wife has these investments, and that should we ever need the money this cushion is there thanks to her."

Live Free or Die

Marital therapists agree that money is a powerful symbol of self-esteem for women. As it has always been for men, money helps women create opportunities for themselves; it is about autonomy and the need to express identity without fear of criticism, judgment, or discussion.

"Money is an arena in which many hidden issues are played out, unbeknownst to a couple," notes Howard Markman, director of the Center for Marital and Family Studies in Denver. "These issues usually involve power, control, status, and trust."

Some women already know this quite well. Having their own money, they say, can actually be good for a re-lationship—a way to avoid battles over *the* most contentious issue in their marriages.

"There are times when I want to buy something that my husband feels is foolish, so rather than fight, I can go ahead and buy it with my money," says Lucille, a partner in a New York marketing firm who has a $10,000 private bank account. "It also helps me feel I have control over my life and adds to my self-esteem, because if the day comes when I am alone—if my husband predeceases me—I will have to manage my money anyway. I don't want to lose touch."

Or, as one politically active woman put it, "If Harold ever knew that I made a $5,000 contribution to Emily's List to support women political candidates, he'd choke. Look at all the aggravation I save him with my secret checking account."

So Don't Feel Guilty! Just Feel Guilty You Didn't Start Sooner!

Remember, money is freedom. It means never having to say "I'm trapped." It means never having to be controlled by some man whose tastes and habits are different from yours, or whose idea of equality is giving you an allowance. Whether you are a homemaker or an executive, no woman is safe without money of her own.

In a 1995 survey of 1,000 professional women by *Working Woman* magazine, 13 percent said they hid money from their husbands. Of those, 43 percent agreed with the statement "I think every woman should have money of her own tucked away"; 30 percent said they used the money for purchases they didn't want to be questioned about; and 25 percent said they did it in case an emergency came up.

54

One of the real surprises is that secret nest eggs and how to sock money away are hot topics of conversation among successful businesswomen who make hefty salaries.

"It's about real independence, about women being able to say, 'I'll meet you next year at that spa in Santa Fe because I've got that Schwab One account,'" says Wendy Reid Crisp, director of the National Association for Female Executives. Wendy freely admits that she keeps money separate from her second husband. Her first marriage broke up after she found herself in a desperate situation when her husband became an alcoholic and almost drank half of the divorce settlement away.

In her speeches to women entrepreneurs around the country, the charismatic executive tells her audiences that there's a need for women to have secret or separate money because modern relationships so often rob couples of their individual privacy.

"Everything is just discussed to death—your work, your sex life, your feelings—and there is a need for some pockets of privacy," Wendy explains. "Stashing money away is always presented as some kind of deceptive thing, but it's really very healthy."

Even Wendy's eighty-four-year-old mom is a pro at this. Since the death of her husband in World War II, when Wendy was a little girl, Maxine has received a monthly check from her husband's old insurance policy. When she remarried some years later, she told her new husband that she gave the check to their church each month. Well, she does, sort of. She cashes the check and then deposits the money in a cigar box she dubs her "Jesus box," from which she has bought gifts for her siblings and her children over the years. Last month, she purchased a new computer and took a class on the Internet. Husband number two could not find Maxine's Jesus box if his life depended on it. Maxine says, "It's buried under piles of clothing in a spare bedroom. Wendy and her brother are the only other ones who know about it."

Even in the liberated 1990s, it seems, women have good reason not to share all of themselves with their men. There are just too many tales of betrayal and hurt. And although dishonesty is not a trait that comes easily to most women, many, in their quiet way, have learned that it's important to look out for their own interests. After all, that's what their mothers told them. And when was your mother ever wrong?

Virginia Kirkpatrick, a businesswoman who sits on a bank board in St. Louis, sees good reason for this—every day.

"There are definitely a lot of men who have secret bank accounts and have their statements mailed directly to their office so their wives won't know. There have been cases where the statement accidentally goes to their home and they come into the bank and throw a fit! The secret accounts are usually checking accounts. They write checks for things they don't want anyone else to know about.

"Some of the men have their statements held at the bank and they pick them up because their wives work in their offices. Some accounts are made in phony names, too, although the bank tries hard not to do that.

"And if there is the smell of divorce in the air, watch out! The first one who gets to the bank is the one to empty the joint accounts. I've seen a wife arrive within an hour or two of her husband and all the money is gone. They stand at the teller's window and weep and curse their husbands."

Or they wise up. . . .

REMEMBER MUD SLIDE SALLY?

Today, Sally's nest egg sits safely—and secretly—in her sister's private safe. Her marriage has come full circle. She filed for divorce from Jeff, serving him the papers while he was on a movie set in Colorado. The detective work it took to find and gather all of their financial documents, as she finally acted in her own behalf, empowered her to confront him about his controlling and selfish ways. She realized that if she had the confidence and strength to get divorced, she had the confidence and strength to be her own person and live free of Jeff's not so benign control. The kids were miserable at the thought of living apart from their loving dad, but mom was determined. After years of cowering, and bending to his rules, she put it to him straight.

"Look, Jeff, I have always lived by your wishes, shopping for bargains, depriving myself and the kids even though we have millions. I realized I can live the way I want to on my own—with half of the divorce settlement. So either I will do that and the children will be affected or you could go to therapy and get help and we can stay together as a family."

He agreed to go to therapy. Sally withdrew the divorce petition. In the months that have followed, Jeff has been doing everything he can to make Sally into his full financial partner. She has met his broker and investment advisers, people whom he always kept secret from her. She started reading up on investment strategies and the stock market and is a much happier and stronger person now. Jeff gave Sally free access to their checkbook—something he had never done before—and she, without feeling too much guilt, bought a new minivan for herself and the kids to replace the beat-up old station wagon with 100,000 miles on it she had been driving. She even splurged on leather seats, which Jeff, of course, had to make a sarcastic comment about. (Hey, no one changes in a day.) All told, Sally was, and continues to be, pleasantly shocked. Could this be the same man she has lived with, counting pennies, for fifteen years?

To Sally's amazement, Jeff has made progress and their marriage is in a much better place. Their kids are happy that most of the tensions are gone.

Asked about his evolution, Jeff says, "Sally made me realize that I had some real deep problems about money. It's not easy to change a lifetime of thinking and habits, but when I saw that I could lose my wife and kids over this, how much was at stake, I knew I needed to change. I realize that I kept all these secrets from her, which is not only harmful to our relationship but not financially smart either. If I died in a plane crash, it would be crucial that she know everything we have and where it is and who my—I mean our—lawyer, broker, and accountant are.

Since I have become more open, a lot of the anger is gone from Sally now, which makes me feel closer to her."

As for Sally's $10,000 nest egg that almost slid into the Pacific Ocean, it has since grown to $40,000 from her monthly deposits and sits in her sister's bedroom safe, protected from the whims of Mother Nature and her husband. Only she and her sister know the combination. And that's how it will stay. But she will invest the $15,000 that Jeff gave her for her birthday. It's a good place to get started.

Jeff, who still calls many of the financial shots in the family and is happy his wife doesn't work, remains in the dark about her nest egg.

"I am glad Jeff and I are making progress and that our marriage is intact," says Sally, sipping orange juice on her deck. "I hope it stays that way. But I will always keep this nest egg and hopefully will make it grow. I have been through very tough times and that money saved my life— and our marriage. It was hard enough emotionally to take that step and seek out a divorce lawyer. I was so frightened and paralyzed for too many unhappy years. It was only because I knew I had that money behind me to hire someone to look out for me that I was able to change my situation.

"That nest egg will always feel like a security blanket," says Sally, who visits her sister and her safe once a month to make a deposit or re-count her cash. Undoing her bathing suit top as she stretched out on her lounge chair overlooking a calm Pacific Ocean, she added, "Look, some women like to visit their old lovers. I like to visit my money."

Twenty Ways to Build Your Nest Egg:
How Do I Hide from Thee? Let Me Count the Ways

Here are some easy, creative, and downright outrageous ways to start and feather that nest egg. Many of these ideas are from women who have been there, done that.

1. Take a part-time job he doesn't know about.
2. If you get paid in cash or make tips, hide the money in the freezer (he'll never find it if he doesn't cook).
3. Rounding off! A new improved way to keep your checkbook balance where only *you* know what's in there. If a bill is $220, round it up to the nearest hundred and enter $300 in the checkbook ledger. If the phone bill is $62, round it off in the checkbook ledger to $80. By year's end you could have an extra $4,000. Take your hubby to Bermuda!
4. Men have poor memories for the little things. Make a list of whoever has to be paid in cash in your household. The guy who mows the lawn, the guy who plows the snow, the gardener, the babysitter, the doorman, the housekeeper. If your husband is the one who pays the bills in your household, every so often tell him these service people have raised their price. Or every other month, say they had to come twice instead of once. "I don't know how that grass grows so fast, Richard!" Or, "Boy, the house gets dirty so quick." Stash it all away.
5. If you have one of those husbands who leaves *all* the parenting to you (there are some fathers who don't even

60

know they have children!), you may be exhausted and frustrated but you can also make out like a bandit. Here's how: Beginning in kindergarten, tell your husband that tuition for Junior's private school is $12,000 a year. Then send him to public school. If your husband hasn't been to a parent-teacher meeting since the Carter administration, how will he ever know? (Think of the fortune you could amass if you have several children!)

6. Open a Swiss bank account.

7. Go to Las Vegas or Atlantic City and tell him you lost it all—except you didn't.

8. Open a secret joint account with a sibling, parent, or trusted friend. While your name is on the joint account, use the other person's Social Security number so no mail or tax documents come to your home. Come tax time, pay your relative or friend whatever tax they will have to pay on the interest your account has accrued.

9. Empty the change or single dollar bills from your purse and his pockets at the end of each day. (Don't forget the shirt pockets.) Put the money in a large coffee can. At end of the month roll the coins, bring them to the bank, and by end of the year you will have money for a vacation for the two of you.

10. Bring your nicest clothes to a consignment shop. Pocket what you sell them for.

11. If your husband is the type who pays your credit card bills but won't share his cash, *charge!* Then resell that expensive stuff to friends. Give them half off if they pay you in cash. It's win-win all around.

12. Or organize luncheons and outings and have friends pay you in cash. Put the tab on his credit card and deposit the cash or checks in your secret account.

13. Anytime a store will give you cash for purchases made on his credit card, *return! return! return!*

14. If you cook, serve him hamburger, not steak. Pocket the difference.

15. Have money from your regular paycheck—or your overtime, commission, or bonus checks—sent separately to your nest egg account.

16. Do you buy lunch every day? Make yourself a sandwich and bring it to work instead of eating out. You will save $20 to $40 a week. *Ca-ching!*

17. Change your tax deduction form at work (W-4) so that you take more deductions or exemptions. Use the extra cash from your paycheck and put it in your nest egg—a mutual fund, savings account, whatever.

18. If you are a full-time homemaker, save money from his paycheck and invest it well. You deserve to get paid a salary for caring for your kids, your home, and him.

19. Wait till he falls asleep. Rifle through his pockets.

20. Does he fall asleep after sex? Have fun—then rifle through his pockets!

(When you get to Chapter 4, you will see how your other half may be hiding money from you. Help yourself to some of those ways too, if that's what works for you!)

2

The Newlywed Game:
Till Checkbooks Do Us Part

The Early and Middle Years

"I always carry something around to remind me of Robert . . . like his credit card."

Every *couple has high hopes in the early* years of marriage. And why shouldn't they? Yet, before much time passes, conflicts do arise—particularly over money. With that in mind, I turned to Ann Landers, one of America's most trusted and experienced voices on love, life, and marriage. She gave me the following words of wisdom to share with women in their twenties, thirties, and forties, including these two gems:

"Any woman who is about to be married or is newly married and who has not discussed how money should be handled is either too young or too stupid to be a suitable life partner."

and

"Always put a little something away for a rainy day— no matter how bright the sun is shining; it won't last."

Another good rule of thumb is to learn your husband's money personality while you're dating. Observe his behavior closely. Ask him leading questions about spending, what he likes to spend on, what he doesn't so you are not surprised, disappointed, or crushed later on.

Particularly in this day and age, when women often live with men or have long relationships before they marry, women have a chance to look at their partner's money philosophy before they take the plunge. "BE VERY, VERY CAREFUL if you see what amounts to a pathology about money," says prominent divorce attorney Myrna Felder. "Because it's only going to get worse once you marry. If this is how he is when he's courting you, imagine when he's got you!"

Just ask Amanda, a twenty-nine-year-old clothing-store manager and newlywed. "Money is the biggest issue in our marriage. We get along great about everything else. It's funny, because at work I tell people what to do all day long. But when I come home, I have to ask Rob: 'Can I buy a blouse for $46?' "

Women also need to be very honest with themselves about money. Are you a good saver? Or does money burn a hole in your pocket? Are you generous or tight with a buck? Did you have big issues around money growing up?

To be sure, marriages are stronger where there is honest communication about how money will be handled in your household early on. "The best thing young people can do for themselves before they tie the knot," advises one of Ivana Trump's matrimonial attorneys, Robert S. Cohen, "is talk about money."

Four Women, Four Lessons

In this chapter, you will hear four women discuss their men, their money, and their marriages. Their stories will show you the radically different ways couples handle money in America and the lengths to which many women go to carve out financial independence for themselves or financial security for their families

Some are more successful than others. Yet they all have a common theme: Women equate money with freedom—the freedom to live by one's own lights, the freedom to make one's own choices, and in the early years of marriage, the freedom to live out one's dreams. The stories of Veronica, Anne, Holly, and Erica also show that it is not enough for a woman to save money. She has to start early if she is going to realize her dreams, with her husband or on her own.

Did you know, for example, that if you took $10 a day from your joint earnings—or $10 from his wallet if you don't work—and you did this every day until you were sixty-five, you could have $434,879* on the day you retired? Now that's financial planning! If you are lucky enough to be among those couples who stay married, think of all the wonderful and extraordinary ways you and your husband can enjoy this pile of dough—money the two of you would never have had otherwise.

Following each woman's true and personal account, you will read an "Observation" section, written in consultation with Sharyn Wolf, the psychotherapist and author mentioned earlier. Wolf is one of the country's leading experts on relationships. (She also has a nest egg.) That sec-

*$3,600 a year at 5 percent compounded interest for forty years yields $434,879.
Source: Melissa Levine, Certified Financial Planner.

tion will analyze both the personal and financial dynamics of the story you will have just read.

The bottom-line message of this chapter is simple: Keep those rose-colored glasses on, girls, for sure. But, meanwhile, do you and your husband this favor: Squirrel money away for those rainiest—and sunniest—of days. And don't completely surrender the financial reins to your husband. Hang on to them, share them with him, but don't let go completely.

Take some words of advice from Bridget Macaskill, president and chief executive officer of Oppenheimer-Funds, Inc. who manages more than $100 billion in mutual fund assets and a woman who advocates women's financial independence:

"You must always believe that one day you are going to have to manage your finances by yourself, because that is the truth. If both of you are going to be working, and both of you are going to be sharing the domestic bills, I'm not saying to keep all your money separate. Keep some of your money in a separate account. Keep some ownership. And have an understanding before you tie the knot about how it's going to work. Some of the other advice I share with young women?

- Don't give up making your own investment decisions.
- Don't give up knowing what his and your financial status is.
- If he wants to file a joint tax return because it makes better sense, fine. Just make sure you understand the return. And when the accountant goes through it, make sure you are there.

- Be there when all joint financial decisions are made. Because for women today, if you never give up being part of the decision-making process, it's never an issue later in your marriage. The real issue is if you have never been part of the money decisions, how on earth do you claim it back? That is much tougher to do."

Veronica:	28 years old
Marital status:	Married 4 years
Job:	Hair colorist
Home:	New Jersey
$$ Strategy:	Hides $20 a day in tips in the freezer

"I hide money from my husband for my husband."

I'm very much in love with my husband. He is lots of fun. We're like little kids together. We can do anything. The one way we are very different, though, is when it comes to money. I'm a real good saver and a careful spender. He buys stupid stuff. He'll pick an expensive restaurant. I'll pick a cheaper one. When we lived together we split all the expenses in half but kept separate accounts. When we married we put all our money together. He got a little greedy. He didn't want me to spend money on clothes. Women's stuff is more expensive than men's stuff. He complained I was spending too much. That's when I started hoarding.

COLD CASH

I picked the freezer so if we got robbed, the money wouldn't be found. But mostly I picked it to hide it from

Tony. I put the envelope underneath my Weight Watchers frozen meals. He doesn't cook so he would never find it. I save $100 a week ($20 a day from my tips). It comes to almost $5,000 a year, which is pretty good, don't you think?

I know I have saved a lot when the Weight Watchers boxes aren't laying right. Then it's time to go to the bank.

I use the money for both of us. I bought our new bed with it. I paid for our cruise to the Caribbean with it. Sometimes I save for our car payment. He'll ask, "Where did you get the money for that?" I don't get into it too much, but he is sure happy that I have it.

So how do I do it?

I wait until he's in bed for the night. I leave money out for him—$20 a day—then I go to the fridge! Every night I go through this charade. I also have a mutual fund he doesn't know about. I have one for us and one for myself. Hey, this is the nineties. You never know what could happen.

SURPRISE, HONEY, I'M (WE'RE) RICH!

And look at the nest egg we are going to have if we make it to our fiftieth or sixtieth wedding anniversary. This money will be for both of us and boy will it be a big and wonderful surprise!

I never tell him the real situation. I always tell him I had a bad day. He thinks I make $30 to $40 a day instead of $100. I'm a good saver, and that's good for our marriage. He buys stupid things like 100 games for his computer, or he wastes it on beer and cigarettes. We have two different money philosophies. He sees the rewards with my system. When I produced the cash I had put aside for our vacation to Disney World, he was amazed and thrilled. He told me: "Way to go! I thought I would spend the whole trip worrying about how we were going to pay for this."

I never want to be destitute. I'm very controlling but I think he likes it that way. He doesn't feel deprived. He thinks he makes more money than I do because he doesn't know about all my tips.

He'd like to cash in half his paycheck and spend it but I make him deposit the whole thing. He's a great person. He has a good heart. He lets me do anything I want, which is probably why we get along so well! I have a lot of freedom and independence. He cleans, does laundry. He's a very easy partner.

The future? We'll have a business, I know that. Maybe a bed and breakfast. We save $2,000 a month—separate from my envelopes, which are mine! We don't have very high bills. I try to live simply so I can have a lot of stuff later.

Observations from the Couch: Sharyn Wolf, CSW

Veronica is doing something wonderful for herself and her husband down the road. It makes sense to save for the future. But there is a tinge of control in their relationship. Is the goal she has shared by him? If you are stashing money to achieve a dream, it's important that the dream be both of yours. Your twenties are the time to buy beers and a few computer games. She needs to make room for him to live his life the way he wants in his twenties. Because what she doesn't want to do is save for a future in a way that deprives him of the joys of being a young man. She needs to look at several issues: Is she trying too hard, in her desire to do something wonderful for both of them? Is she depriving him in ways she doesn't realize, and will there be some negative impact to what she is doing by the time they are in their forties?

Observations from the Financial Couch

Job well done! Hide from your husband for your husband. Veronica knows the value of a dollar and how starting young is the best thing you can do for the two of you. The younger you are, the easier it will be to accumulate the money necessary to make your dreams come true. Having a goal is so crucial, and she has one. It is easier to save money for something specific you want than for an unidentified "ideal." If you and your husband want your dream so intensely, only a true emergency should keep you from diverting the amount you set aside every week or month to fund your nest egg. In the meantime, Veronica, make sure your money doesn't freeze in the freezer; get it to a mutual fund and watch it grow!

Anne:	35 years old
Marital status:	Engaged to George, 30, a New York City policeman
Job:	Computer systems analyst
Home:	Lives in Queens in a 2-bedroom apartment; not planning on kids, they have 4 dogs

And Other Time-Honored Ways to Build a Nest Egg

$$ Strategy: Gives George a $10-a-day allowance for subway fare and snacks. Puts everything else he and she earn in the bank.

"If George had $100 in his pocket, he would eat it in doughnuts and coffee. No way I'm gonna let that happen!"

George and I met seven years ago in Dunkin' Donuts, of all places. I was on my way to a book club and I got lost. I stopped in there for directions. He started talking to my friend and wound up coming to the book club meeting with us because I wouldn't give him my phone number. My friend thought this was funny but I was mortified.

He persuaded me to go out for coffee, and eventually we got to talking and we really hit it off. One of the things he liked about me (aside from my blue eyes) was my bank account! I had been working and saving since I was fourteen, starting with baby-sitting jobs. By the time I was twenty-eight, when we met, I had close to $40,000 in the bank.

He was very impressed. He told me that he once saved $3,000 and was very proud of himself for that. "My god, I am such a loser compared to you! How did you do that?"

What can I say? I am a very determined person when I want something, like a house. I've worked three jobs, the holidays at Christmas in Macy's, whatever I could do to make extra money. Buying a house has been a dream since I was a kid. And next year it looks like between my money and George's (I have squirreled away $20,000 from his paychecks over the last seven years) we are finally going to have a house! He is thrilled about our nest egg. He never thought a house was in reach for us.

The key is hard work and being stingy with myself. I am willing to make do with one pair of black shoes, not twelve, like a lot of women. I'm thinking about not having a traditional wedding either. Feed all those strangers dinner and pay $1,000 for a dress? I'd rather elope and keep the cash in the bank for the house.

George was so blown away by what a good saver I was he instantly turned over his financial affairs to me. Smart guy. He saw that we had been in the workforce the same number of years. I had $40,000 and he had ZERO in the bank.

I make his breakfast and lunch and give him $10 a day in case he wants to buy something. But he usually comes home with that same $10 in his pocket. But if he had $100 in his pocket, he and I both know he would come home with $1. The rest of the money would go for doughnuts, newspapers, gum. I see myself as saving him from himself.

Another way I get money into our nest egg is his uniform allowance. He gets $800 a year to buy and dry-clean *three* uniforms. I say buy two and I'll wash them myself. His income tax refund? He never sees it. I put it right in the bank. If he knew what he was getting back, he would be dangerous with the money. He works hard, too, and I would hate to see his money go to waste.

I also handle all the bills and he is thrilled because what man likes to do paperwork? I do all the budgeting for food shopping, laundry, gas bills—everything. It's like second nature to me. We splurge on going out to eat once a week to a really nice place and we take nice vacations.

But when bills come due, like his tuition bill, he is so thrilled I have the money put away for it. Before George met me, all his bills were late, he missed payments, he had poor credit. Now he is proud of his new credit. He respects my ability to do all this and we both trust each other. It works well.

My sister, who is going through a bitter divorce now, tells me it's good that I trained George early. She wished she had done the same with her husband. He has walked off for another woman with whatever money they had, leaving her and their four kids groveling. For twenty-two years with this man, she never even knew what they had. She trusted that he was putting money away for both of them and now she has no money and rusty job skills since she took herself out of the employment market fourteen years ago to raise their kids. She feels like a fool.

Watching what she is going through makes me all the more determined and glad I have been a disciplined saver, or hoarder! The first bill I pay every month is a check to my savings account. One thing I haven't done is take the time to learn about the stock market. It is a little intimidating and I'm not big on taking chances. I have the maximum going into my retirement 401K, but that's about it. I need to educate myself so I feel safe enough to plunge in.

Oh, one other thing. . . . If your husband is ATM happy like my George, make sure there is no ATM card attached to his account. And insist that he drink his morning coffee at home if he is tempted to stray outside to Starbucks. Even Dunkin' Donuts charges $1.50 for a large. Better the money should go toward a house.

Observations from the Couch: Sharyn Wolf, CSW

For someone else, this might seem like control. But George does not feel humiliated or deprived. He feels fortunate to have a wife who is willing to go to these lengths. Anne is determined to save money for their dreams. She doesn't feel critical of George for being the way he is. In terms of what they want for their lives, she is better equipped to handle this than he is and he agrees. What is important in terms of handling money together for partners is to realize their strengths and weaknesses. When both partners agree, it's a love connection. It's when they don't agree that problems arise.

Observations from the Financial Couch

You are a model of nest egg wisdom and savvy. Many women would be wise to take a page from your book. Just don't forget to have a good time, too, spending money on smaller things that would bring a smile to your face or George's!

Holly:	35 years old
Marital status:	Married 14 years and has 2 children
Job:	Self-described "domestic goddess"
Home:	Miami
$$ Strategy:	"Pay" the same phone or utility bill three times each month. Record the checks in the checkbook ledger as

Florida Power & Light when, in fact, two of the checks
are written to yourself. Also, save allowance money.

*"My husband has the first and last word
when it comes to money. I feel like a maid with a Jaguar."*

I've never felt like I was equal or a partner because my
husband earned the money. He had everything, and he's a
lot older than I am. I always thought that if we split up I'd
probably be leaving on a Schwinn bicycle, no matter how
much money we had, no matter how well we have done
financially. I call myself "a maid with a Jaguar"—meaning
that I have everything in life but it's only good as long as
we are married. I know what would disappear if we
weren't. (We separated twice before, and when that happened, the housekeeper, in fact, went, and the Jaguar was
traded in for a Hyundai.)

The more years we put into this marriage, the more
respect I'm getting as far as a partnership is concerned. I
mean, he'll ask me my opinions about things. But I know
the bottom line about MONEY: I can't buy a car for myself without him. He gets the last word because he makes
the money. And I have to respect that.

So this was my trick for getting money beyond the
$300-a-week allowance he gave me . . . until I was caught.
It was the most devious thing I've ever done.

I'd write checks three times a month in our checkbook
ledger to Florida Power & Light, the utilities company.
Those air-conditioning bills can sure get big in our hot,
sticky, Florida summers! But two of those checks were bo-

gus and were really going to me! And he'd never look at
the canceled checks when they came in the mail—only
the checkbook register. Clever, huh? For a while.

And like many husbands, mine only knew HALF of
what anything cost! It's many women's way. He'd say:
"That's a great dress!" And I'd tell him I got it on sale for
only $100 when it really cost $200. In the end, this didn't
give me real control when it came to money. I always
knew that he truly had the last word. With us, I will never
have the last word on how money is spent.

All of this funny stuff ended when Rick put our checkbook on the computer. In place of carbon-copy checks
and the register you record, he computerized everything.
Now, every check I write is entered into a computer, so
I'm really screwed. Rick did this to get more control over
our checkbook, and so he now knows exactly what I'm
spending. So how did I get into this money mess to begin
with?

BEING DADDY'S LITTLE GIRL CAN BE COSTLY
FOR ALL

When we got married, I was nineteen and he was thirty-
one. I worked with him for several years in his limousine
business but basically I went from college to marriage. I've
never really had to work because he made enough money.

My husband is from the old school. As soon as he met
me, he bought me a car, he paid off my school loans. His
generation is different from people nowadays. Today,
men go for Dutch treat. But he always wanted to take care

of a woman. He wouldn't mind if I had a career, even though I never figured out what I wanted to be when I grew up. I have career fantasies all the time, picturing myself dressed up in a suit, carrying a briefcase and walking into an office every day. But I really became co-dependent with him and his money.

Now I am raising my daughter to work and earn her own money. It's good for any woman to know she is capable of making a living. It's imperative for her self-esteem. Without it, you become a co-dependent person, and I think that's true of any woman.

LIFE ON THE DOLE

So now my husband gives me cash—$300 to spend on whatever I want. This has nothing to do with groceries or the kids. Whatever I don't spend out of the $300 I squirrel away to buy gifts for him, or for friends, and that's okay with him.

Money can create a rift between a couple; it can create bad feelings. I often wonder what would happen if he ever left me. On a rainy day, I might look damned good with all my clothes, but I won't have any cash to buy dinner. My friends are always saying to me: "Why are you spending money on clothes? Just put the money away!"

Observations from the Couch: Sharyn Wolf, CSW

It sounds as if Holly is really angry, so she has to put one over on Rick. It also sounds like her behavior is a continuation of being a little girl. When you are a little kid,

80

it's like being a member of a cult, it's a dependency train-ing ground. Being this little girl helps her feel safe. It's not about the money. She has to fool him. Everything has got to be secret. She has created her own little drama.

There is also a real possibility that Rick knows exactly what he got with Holly. Remember, it takes two in a mar-riage. Some of the questions Holly needs to ask herself are: What piece of herself has she given up in exchange for this tenuous lifestyle? Why does she feel like a maid with a Jaguar, which is a terrible self-image, rather than a partner with a Jaguar? What needs does she have that aren't being met? She has to look at how she can feel more equitable in this relationship to help her not feel like a sneaky little girl. He is the adult; she is the child. That is the deal they made when they got married. He may be satisfied; she is not. If she were to wake up tomorrow like a woman with a Jaguar, instead of a maid with a Jaguar, what would happen differently for her, for them?

Money is the manifestation of power for this couple—how to feel more powerful in the marriage. But, here, it has a lot more to do with her own identity. It still may be a good idea for her to tuck some money away, but in a different way than how she has been doing it. My advice to Holly and to women in a similar situation is that it is more impor-tant for her to work on her identity, and find a way to feel more like a partner to her husband instead of a maid.

View from the Financial Couch

Time to get a job. You'll feel better about yourself. Work gives a woman—a person—a feeling of self-worth.

And Other Time-Honored Ways to Build a Nest Egg

No amount of clothes or shopping will do that. Invest what you have saved instead of buying so many material things. Make it fun. Start shopping instead for stocks with your daughter!

Erica:	34 years old
Marital status:	Married 10 years to a neurosurgeon; 1 daughter, age 5
Job:	Artist
Home:	Philadelphia
$$ Strategy:	Tries to maneuver her husband into paying more of the bills

"We both play this game—I jockey to get him to pay for more things in our life. He jockeys to pay less. Sometimes it's humorous. Sometimes it's not. Steve's not a bad guy, just a tight guy."

Stephen and I dated for three years before we married, and yes, I did observe his "money personality." This is a second marriage for both of us. He always picked up the check. But he was always a little cheap. He'd ration out the number of nice places to funky places. You could see him clicking on—"I want to keep her so I better blow some bucks now!"

I was amused. I saw that it was hard for him to spend often, even for himself. I am still crazy about him after all these years; we love art and music and cherish our daughter. It's just this money thing that still gets me. Steve has this conception that he is still struggling, even though he has plenty. It's just a mindset that he can't get out of. Our vacations aren't bad, although we spend a lot of time going to the in-laws'. Why? Because it's free!

SEPARATE BUT NOT EQUAL

One mistake I probably made when we discussed how money would be handled in our marriage was that we both wanted to keep things separate. I wanted to maintain my own identity—like my name—as well as my own money. His reason: He probably realized he could keep more that way! It worked out better for him. I think Steve would have gone along if I'd said I wanted to put most of my salary in the bank and have him—with his much bigger salary—support us.

The thinking was that it should be based on income, but it hasn't turned out that way. Now I find it's really hard to go back to him and try to renegotiate our arrangement. I used to help pay the mortgage, then I got angry and stopped giving him $1,200 a month toward that. I pay for the groceries, the maid, our daughter, and my clothes. He pays for our insurance, the gardener. I don't even know how much money he has saved or what he has in stock options. He won't tell me!

So, given our setup, we are constantly jockeying over who will pay for what. Ridiculous, isn't it? For example, I won't go to the butcher if I've ordered an expensive roast. I'll send him to pick it up so he'll pay. He knows exactly what I'm doing. Another thing is that I would like a new kitchen. We could use it and we can certainly afford it. Since that is a big-ticket item that he would have to pay for, and it is not important to him, I have to wait until he thinks we need a new kitchen. It's true that I could pay for it myself if I had to, but I won't, on principle.

83

Let's take a moment to be a fly on the wall of Erica's brain. Rarely does a day go by during which she is not having an argument in her head or mentally shadowboxing with her husband over money. What drives her nuts is that as a surgeon, Stephen earns four times what she does. This, she says, is a typical example of what goes on inside her head.

7 A.M.: First thing I say to myself when I wake up in the morning is "I need new sheets." Second thought: "But I'm not going to pay for them!"

1 P.M.: If it's the weekend and I am at the grocery store, I think to myself: "I would love to have steak tonight, but I'm paying so we'll have hamburger." Or if I'm feeling really pissed off at him because he won't have the basement refinished, which is badly needed, I won't buy what he likes to eat if it's too expensive. I know he loves Häagen-Dazs ice cream but I'm not paying four bucks for fancy ice cream when I go to the store. I'll get him a popsicle instead.

6 P.M.: When I come home from work, I'll be straightening up the house, making dinner, and I'll think, "I should get paid for this! I'm working and doing the cleaning and shopping. And doing the child care. I bathe and read to my daughter every night. I put her to bed."

10 P.M.: Bedtime. I'm exhausted. The last thought in my head as I drop onto the pillow is—you guessed it!:

"God we need new sheets! But I'm not paying for them."
Like most men, Steve would sleep on a napkin—his Cal-
dor sheets from his bachelor days. I blow up over this
every two months or so.

What's funny about all this is that in all honesty I
would be just as cheap as he is if I were earning the big
bucks. I would not be opening up my purse to him at all! I
understand how he is operating, I just don't appreciate it!
We are really quite similar about money—a little too
tight. I just want one of us to cave so we can enjoy ourselves a little more and I don't want it to be me.

We laugh about this a lot. We do get along in so many
ways and are each other's best friend. It's just this money
thing neither of us can get past.

He could be spending money now on buying a second home, a bigger house for us (we live in the smallest
house, a modest two-bedroom house in one of the most
affluent Pennsylvania suburbs). As our daughter gets
older, especially as a teenager, this house will be too
small for her and for us. But retirement is his big priority.
He is saving millions for his old age. I think he doesn't
realize that this is a mindset that won't go away, and that
when he gets to sixty-five he still won't be able to
change and feel free about spending. I just think if he
loves me he would spend money on the things that mean
a lot to me.

Given his income—he makes three to four times what
I do—he probably should be paying for more. Beyond
that, he should be willing, when he is paying, to take into
account my desires—like wanting the basement of our

house refinished now, not two years from now. But since he is paying, he picks the time, not me.

I have a little nest egg but not that much, which is probably dumb. I figure since we are going to be million-aires in our retirement, since that's all my husband saves for, I will be okay. I should be putting away more.

Observations from the Couch: Sharyn Wolf, CSW

Erica is depriving herself of things she wants on a principle that is hazy, at best. If Steve is not going to give her money to redo the basement or the kitchen, let her spend her own money, knowing they will retire well. Maybe she can ask him to pay half. If he is still stingy and won't cooperate with her, counseling is in store for these two. Because this is a power struggle, not a marriage. By the same token, he should be more generous given his in-come and not be secretive about what he actually has. There is some investment these two have in her not be-ing provided for and him not disclosing how much money he has.

If they could join forces and agree to be an economic team, they could enjoy much more of their life and their money and really have some good times. One thing Erica can do to renegotiate the arrangement she has with Steve is to say the following:

"This arrangement of keeping our money separate was something I wanted to do when we first got married. It's not working for me in the way I had hoped. I've changed. Our lives have changed. I want to redo this."

It is also time for Erica to insist that Steve disclose

how much money he really has and where it is. Change doesn't come all at once. She can start there and hopefully he can eventually be persuaded to spend more. Their relationship is not getting better as long as she feels deprived and does not confront him with her true feelings. They have to deal with this.

View from the Financial Couch

Erica needs to get over her timidity and insist that Steve tell her what all of his assets are (and vice versa) so that if tragedy should strike, she knows where everything is and can be well-informed. She needs to get the names and phone numbers of his broker, accountant, lawyer, etc.

Erica also should be putting more money away in her own nest egg, in case of a rainy or a sunny day. She is leaving herself too vulnerable and it doesn't have to be that way since she is a professional and a fairly good wage earner herself.

Erica should just stop paying all those household bills, like the groceries or the housekeeper or whatever. She has to stand up to her husband on the grounds of fairness and equity if nothing else. This man with his giant salary should be paying much more of the household bills. How they divide up what to pay for should be calculated by what he makes compared to what she makes. If she did that, she would have a lot more leftover from her own paycheck to squirrel away. End of discussion!

General Financial Tips for Your Twenties and Thirties

- Have a cash reserve, an emergency cushion that covers three to six months' worth of living expenses should you lose your job or your husband, or should you get sick. This money should be liquid—like cash or a CD, not tied up in investments—so you can get your hands on the cash quickly if you need it.
- Stay out of credit card debt. Do not live beyond your means!
- Get in the habit of keeping your financial records organized.
- Take the fullest possible advantage of retirement savings plans, like 401Ks and IRAs.
- In terms of investing, because you are young lean toward stocks.
- Try to save 10 percent of your salary every year. Have money automatically deducted from your paycheck. Don't wait until your forties to start saving!
- Don't overlook the importance of a will. A will ensures that for both of you, your finances, property, and family will be taken care of exactly as you wished, heaven forbid something should happen to you. Without a will, the government can decide how to dispose of your money, even who'll be appointed guardians of your minor children. Yikes!
- Don't forget health insurance. Make sure you are covered through your job, your husband's job, or by a private policy for yourself. One serious illness can drain you of every penny you have, and then some.

3

Bad Guys

The Middle Years

"As a matter of fact, you did catch us at a bad time."

O *many women are left holding the bag—an* empty one—when husbands go through their midlife crisis and leave for another woman, or just become impossible to live with. Don't get caught short. This chapter will help you plan for this day should it come.

One woman who understands this better than most is Olivia Goldsmith, author of *The First Wives Club*. You remember the movie—where Goldie Hawn, Bette Midler, and Diane Keaton got mad and then got even with men who had dumped them for younger women. Who better to talk about the pain and anger wives experience when their husbands turn out to be card-carrying members of that nefarious Bad Boys club? So we talked over lunch, at a cozy Manhattan bistro.

First she spoke about her own experience with her husband (now her ex) and money. This was before she was a best-selling author and screenwriter. Like most of us, she was sorry she did not have a nest egg put away. She was young—twenty-nine at the altar, thirty-five in divorce court.

"Okay, I wasn't calendar young, but I was emotionally young," she said, laughing. "We never, never, *never* discussed money before we married. It was a big mistake."

The marriage, she said, lasted six years and took another seven years and $60,000 in legal fees to get out of. One big reason? Her former husband liked to spend every penny, while she wanted to save.

"I remember finally selling my business and having a nest egg and saying I really wanted to keep this money together, safe, so that someday I could quit working and maybe write.

"He said: 'I want to buy matching coyote parkas.'

"I said: 'Hello???' He wanted to blow $20,000 on two ski parkas out of coyote fur? Never mind the political correctness of this! This was my blood money! It had taken me a whole lifetime to be good enough to have a business that had some equity in it. No! Not *coyote parkas!* I think we work too hard for our money to not think of it as freedom.

"We never talked about money when we first met. He knew from the beginning that I earned plenty. He liked the benefits of that. But he also wanted me to stay home and cook for him. Need I say more?"

After *The First Wives Club* came out, Goldsmith said she received thousands of letters from women who found themselves victims of their husbands' atrocious betrayals. They wrote from all over the country, all over the world, to vent.

"Can I tell you some horror stories?" Goldsmith asked, leaning over her frittata.

"One woman wrote telling me about what she thought was a good marriage. She loved her husband.

They were married more than thirty years. He fell down on the kitchen floor with a heart attack—I'm talking real cardiac arrest. She did the breath of life or whatever it's called into his lungs for forty minutes. The emergency services guys came and said: 'Forget it! He's a goner!' She kept breathing into him. She resuscitated him. He came back. Six weeks later, he is back at work. He is okay. He calls her to say he is not coming home that night or ever. He is leaving her for his secretary.

"In the six weeks since he had recovered, he had had a life-changing experience and decided to reassess his life. Not telling her, he put every bit of their funds—including taking another mortgage out on the house for the extra cash—in an offshore account in the Cayman Islands. And he left. She wrote me and said: 'I WISHED HE HAD DIED ON THE FLOOR! I would have been a wealthy, respected widow instead of a penniless, humiliated divorcée.'

"I'm giving you the worst-case scenarios," she told me, flagging the waiter for another Diet Coke, "where women felt perfectly secure and had no indication that anything was wrong. They said, 'It can't happen to me.' Well, it can happen to anybody! Trust me!"

DR. JEKYLLS AND MR. HIDES

What follows are the stories—told in their own words—of four women who loved their husbands, trusted that they would be there for the long haul, and had that trust betrayed. You will also get extraordinary advice from renowned New York matrimonial attorney Myrna Felder. Everyone should have a lawyer like her!

This chapter is not to make you paranoid. It's just to show you that this can, and does, happen to anyone. We never really know whom we are living with. And life's twists and turns can change even the most stable and trusted person we have called our mate for years. You can be the best wife, the best friend, the best possible partner in the world. But life and marriage can be unpredictable, even cruel. So you need to be protected—not by the man in your life, but by you! Hopefully this will never come to pass in your marriage, but look around. We all know someone who has had the sky fall in on them. Right? If only they had had a nest egg of their own—their own money and power—to sustain themselves and their family, their journey through one of life's most difficult passages would have been so much easier.

Shelley:	51 years old
Marital status:	Divorced after 12 years of marriage to a network television executive
Job:	TV journalist
Home:	Washington, D.C.
$$ Strategy:	None. She gave him everything she had.

"In order to avoid confusion, I grasped at the loving straw."

I was in my thirties, a very successful TV journalist making a six-figure income as an anchorwoman in a major television market. I was sure I knew everything. My mindset was, "nothing bad can happen to me."

I married an older man who had been married before. He is a well-known guy in network television, terribly charming, and I was incredibly attracted to him. But . . . he had two children from his first marriage—ten and twelve years old and an angry ex-wife. I wasn't really paying attention. There was love, love, love. I really used the opportunity to put my domestic life in order—or so I thought. I had neglected everything else in my life since I was so devoted to my career. He and I agreed that for our marriage to work, togetherness was essential. So I phased out my all-consuming career in order to phase in a more balanced new life. I no longer wanted to do this fast-track, repetitive, high-pressure job and be away from my husband. I wanted to travel with him when he traveled and enjoy my time with him. When we were dating, I'd be in Los Angeles, for example, covering the mayor's race. He would fly in for business. We'd meet at a hotel—it was delicious. We wanted to see more of each other, so we got married and moved to the suburbs. His first wife was not well, so I became a mom to his kids, who needed lots of special attention following their parents' bitter divorce and their mother's illness. I put the kids' needs first and we created a real family feeling during our twelve years of marriage. My husband could often be very loving, taking me onto his lap and hugging me like a protected little girl. And I made the big mistake of trusting him with my financial future.

How did we handle the money?

I came to the marriage with assets well over $250,000. I owned a house and also had $100,000 in cash. We were supposed to have his, mine, and ours. A lot of his money, however, got subdivided from his first divorce. He was a very responsible dad. He paid for all the private schools, etc. I understood he had a huge financial commitment on his side.

MISTAKE NO. 1

Everything I had I put into our joint account. My paycheck, my hard-earned $100,000 savings. I started a business out of the house, which helped us write off a lot of taxes. When I had big losses, he got huge tax benefits from my business. Everything I did in our marriage enhanced our lifestyle. I loved his kids, took them to school, took them to look at colleges when they got older.

We bought a long-neglected, Victorian house to refurbish. I did much of the work myself—sanding, scraping, painting, refinishing the floors. I put my heart and soul into that house. Sweat equity and lots of my own money, too! He insisted on buying the house right before our wedding—for "tax purposes" he said—and didn't put my name on the deed. Whenever I asked him about that, he would say: "Oh, I'll get around to it when I'm not so busy." Then he'd explode: "Why are you in such a rush to put your name on the house? Are you planning the divorce already?" Being a real people pleaser, I always tried to settle him down, hoping it would work itself out. He always called it "our house"—until the divorce. Then it became his house. He got it in the settlement.

After a time in our marriage, I did freelance reporting. But each time I left to go report a story, he would make a

big scene about me "leaving the family," and he was jeal-
ous that I was working with other men—even the film
crew. So rather than fight, I turned down a lot of jobs. I
got very cozy instead in my little world with him and his
children.

I came to see he was money and power oriented. Or, in
the words of Oscar Wilde, "A man who knows the price of
everything and the value of nothing." Anything I did out of
his sight, I was accused of having affairs, which I never
had. He's one of these men who's so charming, sweet, and
funny, with a self-deprecating sense of humor—until he
snaps. Then he goes over the wall. And afterward, he has a
little boy's ability to make you feel sorry for him!

As the marriage went on, I knew things were being
bought and not being put in my name. I didn't want to
fight over that—I told myself I'd deal with that later!
When I did question him, he would yell: "What are you in
this for? The money?" He would always say: "It's in my
name but it's both of ours!"

I ONCE WAS BLIND BUT NOW I SEE

Now, of course, I see clearly what was happening, but I was
blind to it then. For a reporter who would, if I had to, even
ask the garbageman to see what people recycled in their
trash, I did only a superficial look-see in my relationship
with this man. Professionally I'm tough, but when it comes
to love, I was dumb. All because I hate confrontation.

For example, his ex-wife came back asking him for
more money. He paid her off in full with *my cash!* He

98

could have done this by selling a very small portion of his stocks and bonds. But, like an idiot, I took $80,000 from my cash reserves and paid her off. He also had separate bank accounts that I didn't even know about until the divorce. He said it was to protect himself.

Then, in 1990, I got colon cancer. That was a wake-up call. Cancer gave me the courage to be really honest about these things. You realize that life is finite. Life with this man had turned into a living hell. He had a volatile temper and I never knew what would trigger it. Suddenly I had kids, but they weren't mine; I had all the responsibility but none of the power. I'm hearing this a lot. Childless second wives married to well-to-do older men are ending up with the kids. . . . I didn't get any financial credit for raising these kids. He was arguing that I should bring in more money. At the same time, he was telling me not to work, to be available to him to travel, and to help the kids maintain their life with their father. He held all the cards and I felt like the servant girl, the au pair. I raise the kids, travel with you, do the entertaining, and I don't even have the status of full partner.

At the end I was pushing him to put my name on stuff. He was willing to let our marriage blow up over the issue of control, the need to call the shots on everything. It was physically making me ill.

THE PRICE OF SILENCE

When the whole thing came down, there were all kinds of assets that should have been jointly owned and a lot of money that disappeared. I'm sure there is money hidden in offshore banks. He would travel to the Caribbean often. I was sure he was going to visit his money. I thought that only stupid women got into financial difficulties. I had all these funny feelings, these suspicions that he was doing things behind my back to weaken my financial position in the marriage. But I hated the emotional fallout from our confrontations—his rage followed by his hostile silence. So I kept the peace by not asking questions.

His game, I later learned, was to pay cash for all the major expenses—cars for his kids, their college tuitions—to drain down the cash so he would look cash poor in case of divorce. Beware when men pay off low-interest-rate mortgages they don't need to pay off. Suddenly he paid off the mortgage on our vacation home. I wondered why. It was at such a low interest rate. He puts down $60,000 to $80,000 in cash. Now the cash that I have access to is dwindling, dwindling. He drained my cash and with it my confidence and the freedom to get out.

He also wanted me to put *his name* on my house! Finally there was somebody at home in my little brain who said, "No!" I realized later why he wanted me to do this. My house was already paid for when I got married. He saw the opportunity to borrow off my house and get more cash for himself. He could pay for his ex-wife's expenses and his kids' educations with the equity in my house!

FIGHTING BACK—FINALLY

I got smart. I got a lawyer. By now, he was no longer scaring me. I would no longer burst into tears. He could tell I had found my strength. I did the therapy and then, in 1994, I did the divorce. I made myself know there was no way to save this marriage. As I felt stronger and stronger, he seized more and more control of our financial assets— closing a joint account without obtaining my signature and canceling our joint credit cards without warning. He had secret conversations with financial people and tried to get his hands on the money in my business account. Thank goodness I had a good attorney who gave me the courage to fight.

When I filed for divorce, he turned on me in a rage! He said I was an evil person. He tried to hold on to everything. He accused *me* of hiding money! It turned out *he* had secret bank accounts with hundreds of thousands of dollars in them. I had put his name on my bank account. He had put my name on his, but he had another bank account that I never knew about.

My lawyer decided not to track down the money hidden in the offshore banks. I got a fair settlement; I could have gotten more, but I wanted to end it.

The whole thing came out right. I got a whole new energy level back. I will never be married again. I don't need to be married again. I prefer to be on my own, but with a man in my life. Since the commingling of money doesn't come up, it makes it a lot cleaner and nicer. When I travel with my boyfriend now, I insist on paying my own way. It feels better.

Words of Wisdom from Divorce Lawyer
Myrna Felder

This is what one of America's most respected divorce lawyers, 101 *Myrna Felder, would have advised Shelley and the three other women who share their stories here. Listen to her words carefully. You or someone you care about may be in these very same shoes right now and could use a helping hand.*

No. 1. IF YOU HAD A NEST EGG BEFORE YOU GOT MARRIED, DON'T COMMINGLE YOUR MONEY OR ASSETS WITH HIS! That way, if you divorce, what was yours before the marriage will be yours after the marriage has ended. Once you commingle your money, with a joint bank account or joint investments, all bets are off for ever claiming your original nest egg back.

No. 2. BEFORE YOU START SCRUBBING THE FLOORS OF THE VICTORIAN FIXER-UPPER, QUIETLY FIND OUT WHAT THE HOUSE WAS WORTH THE DAY YOU MARRIED HIM. You may not be able to share in the value that the house had on the day you married him, but you will probably be entitled to share in however much the property you worked so hard on increases in value during the marriage. You need to be able to tell the court what the house was worth before you said "I do." If your husband bought the house just before the marriage, the purchase price proves what the value is. And he probably has documents in connection with the purchase. If not, you can quietly hire an appraiser and get the house appraised. I'm very much in favor of things that can be done without making too much noise about it and alerting the other side. It's all very well and good to give advice, but many times it's very hard for women to withstand what their husband is going to do in reaction. So the less they know about your little self-help projects, the better.

102

No. 3. WHEN THE EX-WIFE COMES ASKING FOR MORE MONEY, DON'T LET HER OR YOUR HUSBAND USE YOUR HARD-EARNED CASH! When there is an ex-wife in the picture, the LESS the ex-wife has dibs on, or knows about the present wife's funds, the better. Because what the ex-wife gets should be based on what the ex-husband has, not what you, the new wife, have! One of the things that would make it easier for a second wife is not being so forthcoming to her husband about what she has. Once a man knows you have that cash sitting there, it's very hard in an ongoing marriage to say no when he wants it.

So how do you keep your husband from knowing you have your own money? Many times a wife will have money in a joint account with her mother or a sibling. That way, your money is not in the picture.

No. 4. DON'T LEAVE YOUR DAY JOB! Women who make their husbands their life's center tend to lose the self-esteem and confidence that you get when you make your own way and your own money. In this country, unfortunately, we measure people by the money they make. And people tend to measure themselves that way, too. Women who earn money and have a career feel differently about themselves. They feel stronger.

When a spouse leaves, it's a devastating event. And part of the devastation is that they're saying to you: "You are not worth anything to me." If you have a career or your own money and, therefore, a good sense of your own self-worth, it's not as hurtful. If you have left the job market, all too often it is a monumental task to try and start a career at a later stage in life.

103

While it's true that a woman who doesn't work may stand a better chance of getting alimony—or "maintenance" as it is now called in most states—and a working woman may not, bouncing back from divorce, either financially or emotionally, is usually much easier for a woman who has her own career to fall back on. She is not so dependent on her husband for her view of life.

No. 5. GET THEE TO A DIVORCE LAWYER WAY BEFORE DIVORCE IS ON YOUR LIPS—WHEN IT'S JUST ON YOUR MIND AS A POSSIBILITY. Many times, by the time women get to a divorce lawyer or file for divorce, a lot of the financial damage has been done and there is nothing more that can be done. For example, a husband may get to the bank and withdraw all the money from your joint accounts before you know what has hit you. So lots of people see me and other divorce lawyers *way before* there is ever going to be a divorce, and get some guidance on how they should conduct themselves on some of these financial issues. For example, in Shelley's case, the minute her husband closed their joint account, instead of begging, she could have gone to the court right then and there and asked for a temporary support order. That would have given her enough money temporarily to substitute for the canceled credit cards. So many times people are so emotionally destroyed that they are not ready to see a divorce lawyer. And what happens is that a lot of damage is done before they can get there.

No. 6. MAKE SURE YOUR NAME IS ON EVERYTHING! SIGN! SIGN! SIGN! (EXCEPT, PERHAPS, THE TAX RETURN!) Make sure your name is on EVERYTHING! The deed to your house, all the bank accounts, stocks, etc. The reasons? Not so much for who gets what in the divorce—the courts in most states generally divide the marital pot, whether your name is on an asset or not. It's to protect your assets while you are married. Because a "bad guy" can drain everything you have built together if that's his game. Without your name on the house deed, for example, he can take out a second mortgage on the house and spend all the cash on his new girlfriend while draining all the equity you have built. If your name is on the house, he can't make any moves without your signature and knowledge.

Don't even think about letting your husband pass off some baloney story or excuse like: "I'm not putting your name on the house for tax purposes" or "Only my name is on the house but it's both of ours!" *Your name is power.*

No. 7. BEWARE OF A MAN WHO'S BEEN DIVORCED BEFORE! He knows the financial ropes and you don't. Knowledge is strength. And if he turns out to be an impossible man to live with who is out to screw you, you'd better be prepared. You can get taken to the cleaners.

No. 8. KNOW THE SCORE! Make him tell you about all of his assets, including his bank accounts, brokerage accounts, investments, etc. If you think he is hiding money from you, watch the mail carefully at home. If nothing comes to your home, he is probably having it sent to his office. Have a look around there when he's at lunch or out of town. Write down all account numbers. Remember: In a divorce, documents are everything!

"Men like to write down what they have," said divorce attorney Robert Stephen Cohen. He's represented such names as Ivana Trump and Marla Maples Trump and he adds: "If your husband has done this, take a Polaroid of the notebook or cocktail napkin where he wrote down how much he is worth. If you make a copy of your spouse's handwriting, you are in a position to prove he has money that he is trying to hide from you."

No. 9. IF YOUR HUSBAND IS PULLING OUT MONEY, GET TO COURT AT ONCE! When you begin a divorce action, if there is any evidence that your spouse might be pulling out money, or stocks, you can ask the court for an injunction while the lawsuit is pending. This will restrain your hubby from removing money, or even from removing stuff from the safe-deposit box! True, that's a declaration of war. But if you really think he is wiping stuff out, remember Munich and Chamberlain. Sometimes a declaration of war is better than trying to make nice. You can really be at a disadvantage if everything is gone by the time the court has a look at your assets.

Meryl: 50 years old
Marital status: Divorced after 25 years of marriage; mother of 2

Job:	President of public relations firm
Home:	Chicago
$$ Strategy:	None. She trusted her husband.

"It was not even on the meter that this could happen to me."

It was August. I was recovering from hip surgery, doing my pathetic little exercises on the living room floor, when Tom dropped a bomb on our lives with four words: "I want a divorce." Allison was thirteen and Andy was eighteen, ready to start his freshman year in college. We had been the perfect nuclear family, with all the comforts you could ask for. I worked as hard as Tom did. I just made much less. There was not one day in our marriage that I did not wake up and put on a suit and go to the office. We had a terrific apartment overlooking Lake Michigan, a house in the Wisconsin lake country, and two wonderful children.

I think Tom went into some kind of depression. I noticed in the last year of our marriage that most of the time when he was in the house he was asleep. He flat out did not go to work. He was a brilliant architect. I kept thinking he must be so brilliant that they didn't mind if he didn't show up. But then it evolved, in fact, that he had a love interest two states away. His office noticed sufficiently. He was kicked out of the firm.

All of a sudden, as of December 31, 1992, his contribution of money to our household disappeared, along with our health, disability, and life insurance, and there were a lot of questions about what the kids and I should do. He left the Saturday after Thanksgiving. His girlfriend—who had sneaked away to Paris with him on a business trip while we were married—drove up to our apartment building and whisked him away in her Lexus.

107

STARTING OVER . . . ALONE

I panicked. My children and my home were on the line. There was a cessation of money. He just left cold, leaving no instructions. It was like "the hell with you all." So I had to make it up as we went along. We had a lot of expenses— ever-increasing school tuitions, mortgages on two homes that had to be met in thirty-day increments. Allison was starting orthodontia and all the usual teenage things that cost money. What, I was going to let her have crooked teeth 'cause Daddy ran away? I don't think so.

Months went by. We had money in the bank and I had my paycheck. But what I didn't have was any sign from Tom as to how he intended to care for his family, who were used to what we were used to. I had no sign from Tom as to how he planned to keep me and the kids financially whole. That is when this fellow said to me: "You've got to protect yourself. Get a lawyer." So I did. Remember, if nothing else I am sensible.

How did our financial lives change?

For the entire twenty-five years of our marriage, we had always been a good economic team. Both of our salaries went into one pot. Everything was jointly held ex-cept for our IRAs. We never got in over our heads. We put money away for taxes. Our only long-term debts were the mortgages. He outearned me by a lot all of our life. So my salary paid for our vacations and the groceries. His salary went for everything else. I managed the money. He made the decisions on the big things.

Did it ever occur to me to have a little nest egg on the side just in case this ever happened? No. It never occurred to me that we were not on this straight and narrow path together *forever.* When his architectural firm collapsed in 1987, that was the first clue I had that I should have put money away for a rainy day. His considerable pension FLAT OUT DISAPPEARED, and it was over six figures. Like it never existed! This was not something we could see coming—it was a large, screwy, architectural firm. We were sucked into paying off the debt of the bankruptcy of the firm. He ended up writing checks for hundreds of thousands of our dollars—including the $5,000 gift my father gave ME every year at Christmas—to pay off his share of the bankruptcy. I would have gotten half of that money for my retirement. Now I will get nothing.

HE GOT THE BLONDE AND THE BANK ACCOUNT

As for my life now, the three of us are living on 20 percent of what we used to live on—$60,000 instead of $300,000. His new wife shares in the fruits of his earnings. And she, I just found out, has quit her job! She doesn't feel like working full-time anymore. So Tom will have the last laugh, there is no question about it. When he went through his midlife crisis and was fired, there was no money coming in so the judge couldn't order him to pay what he didn't have. I just got a fixed rate of child support, no alimony. He even refused to take out disability insurance to make sure the kids were protected in case he couldn't work and send child support. "Nothing is going to happen to me," he snapped, as if I was stupid to even raise the issue. In theory, we should have been worth more than $1 million today. If I were a younger woman today, I would definitely learn at a much earlier age how the stock market works. I would definitely have carved out money for the kids and myself. Tom's point of view the whole time was that we would always go on. All four of us had the routine expectation that this—our lives together as a family—would go on forever. But he pulled out and left us. The man took his suits and his books and disappeared from our lives!

My biggest fear was for the kids. They were in private schools and I didn't want to take that away from them or any opportunities that came their way. Tom would have. This wouldn't have been on his meter at all as important. If we had to move to the farm to live with my parents, he wouldn't have cared. He could live on nothing. He just wanted out.

As for myself, once the kids leave school, my life will change cataclysmically. I will get nothing. He did leave me the apartment, which I pay the mortgage on. I got screwed bigger, because my capacity to earn is not as great as his, with his professional degree. When his pension was raided, I lost the means to get that money back.

While I have worked steadily, I don't have a credential, a professional degree, like he does. I have no claim to his professional degree. No claim on his future earnings.

He could make $5 million while married to Miss Goldilocks and I would get nothing. He is scot-free and my future—my old age—is not financially secure or certain. I am frantic about having too small a cushion for my golden years, wondering how I will, as the only breadwinner, support myself. You know, it's not just aging actresses who have to worry, it's aging women in general whose economic opportunities start to decline.

I Could Kick Myself for Not Being Smarter

Now of course I wish I had stashed money away. My mother went to her grave being totally protected by my father. It doesn't happen that way anymore. My advice to my daughter will be to tell her to save separately, but not secretly. Figure out who kicks in what to the joint expenses and the savings. It's incumbent on a woman to know how money operates. I have a childhood friend who didn't even have a checkbook in her name. When her husband put a gun to her head in her basement, she figured it was time to get out and she didn't even know how to write a check. I think her father bailed her out so she could keep her house!

My day-to-day life has changed, too. I can't travel as much. There are no extras anymore for me. I can't do some of the things for Allison that I would like. I don't eat out. I very rarely buy clothes. It's a good thing I bought my silk blouses in the eighties. It's breaking my heart that I have to put our summer home up for sale. There are so many memories in that place, the summers with the kids.

But it is too much of a weight for me financially. I'm also selling some art for small amounts of money. I don't want to sell my grandmother's jewelry. I really look at every aspect of my life now as if it's fungible.

My life is moving forward, but more slowly. I've put off making some sound financial decisions, like not selling the house in the country sooner because there is so much emotion attached to it. It makes me seethe to think I have to sell this because of him. There is also a part of me that is living in a dream world . . . thinking that he will come through and I won't be left with money insecurities.

My anger is focused more on what he did to the kids than on what he did to me. Tom gave Andy the news in the stairwell of his dorm, just a few months after he'd started his first year in college. Andy had to work this out with the student resident adviser on his floor. Then when Allison ordered her high school ring, he wouldn't kick in half, which broke her heart. I go around the bend when I think of this. So I'm focusing on the kids rather than on taking care of me. I still haven't swung around to figuring out me yet—at least in terms of finances.

In the end, I think my anger over Tom leaving has done two things:

It has made me not believe in anything anymore. I'm totally wary of relationships, that anything good can come out of them. I'm not seeing the benefit of being allied with a man. I thought the team concept was there. We both went out to work and we did it. But I got the shorter end of the stick than I needed to have gotten.

And also, I have to say, even though my life is very

stressful, I walk down the street and think: "I am *so lucky not* to be married to that man anymore!"

**Words of Wisdom from Divorce Lawyer
Myrna Felder**

No. 1. MERYL SHOULD HAVE GONE TO A LAWYER RIGHT AWAY, INSTEAD OF LETTING MONTHS GO BY AFTER HE LEFT. She could have gone right to court for support for herself. Why is it important that women in this situation do that? Because most courts cannot make awards of financial support for the time before the divorce action began. They can only give you maintenance (alimony) or child support from the time you file with the court. A lot of women are lulled into thinking, even with lawyers, that they'll work something out; they want to do this the nice way. They don't want to get the court involved and they end up losing a piece of time that is really critical. The lesson here: As soon as his girlfriend pulls up to the house to whisk away your soon-to-be ex-husband, go to court and get some monetary support right then!

No. 2. MAKE SURE YOUR LAWYER GETS A SETTLEMENT AGREEMENT THAT INCLUDES YOUR HUSBAND'S FUTURE EARNINGS IF HE CONVENIENTLY HAPPENS TO BE UNEMPLOYED AT THE TIME OF THE DIVORCE. Meryl's was a very difficult situation to be in. Her husband had stopped working. What often happens is that these men rise like a phoenix from the ashes. So you try to get an agreement that goes like this: Later, if your income rises, I should have the same percentage of your earnings as I am getting now. So if it is 20 percent of his earnings now, it will be 20 percent later, when he is doing well again. Of course, your husband has to agree to that. You should also know that if he files for bankruptcy, he is still on the hook for child support and maintenance.

No. 3. BRUSH YOURSELF OFF AND START OVER. TRY TO GET RID OF THE ANGER. IT'S POISON.

Donna:	41 years old
Marital status:	Divorced and remarried; walked out on abusive first husband on eighth wedding anniversary; 2 children
Job:	Director of New Life, a nonprofit group for abused women
Home:	North Carolina
$$ Strategy:	None

"He would buy my clothes. He even bought my sanitary stuff.
Just to keep me away from that money. . . . I was told
it was not good for me to handle money
because I was dumb and naive."

I married because I was a teenage mother. I was eighteen. I had a one-year old daughter with him and everyone was saying to me: "You need to marry this man because you wanted to have a baby by him and you are not going to do any better." That type of thing. My family was real stern that he had to take care of this baby and me. He was twenty-three. Monies were not plentiful.

I think he already had some abusive tendencies, but the lack of money pushed him to the edge and caused him to be not such a nice person. I would often have to go to my mother's house to eat. He'd pay for what he wanted to eat, but I had to eat what was in the house whether it was good for me or not. She would say: "As long as you are eating, be happy. Even if it's beans." My mother was from the old school. We never knew we were poor until we read the papers!

We were in a good marriage for a whole year. I worked part-time as a nurse's aide. He worked as a maintenance worker for public housing. And he had some part-time jobs. He made okay money. I didn't see any of it. And what little I made I had to turn over to him.

FIRST SIGNS OF TROUBLE

I really had to struggle around me buying myself simple things, like panty hose. I remember that when we got paid every two weeks, I would not even cash my check. He said that was wrong for me to do. He handled the bills. I was told it was not good for me to handle money because I was dumb and naive.

I learned how to survive. When my bras wore out, I would figure out ways to pin the worn-out straps to my clothes to hold me up. I would also save all of my panty hose. The leg that was ruined, that had a run it, I would cut off. Then I would wear the good legs of two pairs of stockings. When I asked him for money for new stockings, he would yell: "BUT I JUST BOUGHT YOU

PANTY HOSE LAST WEEK!" I had to go to him for everything. There was no such thing as an allowance. He handled everything.

I felt so trapped and humiliated. But I stayed in the relationship so long because at least I was barely surviving; I thought if I left I wouldn't survive. The older ladies in the community told me to just stay there and deal with it. They would try to teach me different methods to deal with him, like ignoring him. They meant well, but that was all they knew.

I know if I had money I would have left. I was trapped in a hateful life with this man because I didn't have a cent to my name. Even if I wanted to put money away to plan for my escape, I had no access to it. When I began to grow up I actually started stealing from his wallet when he went to sleep. Every now and then he would ask: "Have you got my money?" I would say no. And he didn't say anything more. He believed me. That showed me he didn't know how much money he had! And he had plenty. He would tuck it away in the bottom of a drawer. Sometimes he would take the drawer out of the dresser and the money he was hiding would drop on the floor and I would pick it up without him seeing.

He also hid money in the mattress. I was being nosy one day. (I would snoop when he was away from home.) Women talked on the talk shows about going under the mattress. I had to think how he thought. I was looking around and I saw that there was a cut in the mattress and he had sewed it back together with pins. I hit the jackpot! I found a couple of hundred dollars! I took a small part of it and then put the money and mattress back the way I'd found it. I bought myself some decent underwear and a new dress. When he asked me where I got it, I said my mother or sister gave it to me.

116

ROCK BOTTOM

It was a horrible marriage. There was such pain in it. He was physically abusive. He needed to grow up bad. I left him on our wedding anniversary, April 3, 1984. I didn't have a dime. I got money from friends and my family to get an apartment. When I told him I was leaving, Roosevelt took every cent of our money out of the bank— about $3,500—and I had no money to buy furniture. I'd thought I could write a check. My daughters and I slept on the floor. That's when I went to the Perdue chicken factory and got a job on the assembly line. For ten hours a day I was on my feet, picking excess feathers off the chicken wings, then I was a draw hand, I pulled out the intestines. It was hard and dangerous work.

But out of all the bad things that happened at Perdue, this was my first full-time job and it taught me how to handle money. I bought us beds and furniture. I was bringing home $180 a week, and I began to learn how to budget money. It wasn't easy but me and the girls did fine according to our standards. We had food, clothing, and, best of all, we had peace. My children are in a much different and better place since we left. My eldest daughter is in college. When I think of how far I have come, I cry. But they are tears of joy. I was so resentful of this man. I

was a hateful beast! And I carried that hate for *sooo* long.
And it has only been in the last couple of years that I have
gone through a healing process for myself and can iden-
tify what that marriage did to me.

In those days, I was attracting all these deadbeat guys.
It was like I was wearing a sign on my back that said:
"DEADBEAT! HERE'S DONNA! PLEASE USE HER!"

Praise God and Pass the Paycheck to Me

Last year I remarried. My new husband is a minister. This
man was just so sensitive to my needs. You know how
women say they pray to God "Just send me this man"? I
couldn't have put together a more sensitive person. He's
not controlling. Both of us trust each other. I'm in school
full-time, and I work part-time.

Money is handled in a totally different way now. He
closed his bank account and transferred everything to mine.
Even his checks now go in my account. He didn't care if his
money was in my name only. I put his name on it.

A girlfriend recently suggested that I have a secret account because I got upset when I found out he'd taken
$200 out of the bank and hadn't told me. Not that I cared
about the money, but he didn't tell me about it. He said he
did, but I know he didn't. My friend said I should put
away $100 or $200 a month. She said, "You never know.
Look how you didn't have a dime last time when your
marriage ended."

So I took her advice. And now I put away $25 every sin-
gle week. I put it in a savings account. He found the pass-

book a month ago. I said I was just saving, that's all. He said, "That's cute!" That was all. So he knows. I'm saving some of what I earn for me and my kids so we can always be whole.

In my job at New Life, I teach women how to feel whole, and that men aren't a life support. That you don't have to have someone come in and abuse you just to say "I have a man." I teach women that you first have to feel good about yourself before you go into any kind of relationship.

Many of the men I have seen even control their girl-friends' money. The men come in the first of the month, say all the sweet things, take their girlfriends' monies, eat up all the food that was bought with their girlfriends' food stamps, and then they are out of there. They may not see them again till the next check comes.

I asked a sister, "Why do you even deal with that?"

"Donna," she said, "you know what? At least I don't deal with total loneliness."

I don't hear from Roosevelt anymore except when we are in court for child support. He goes six, seven months not paying and then I have to haul him into court. I don't depend on his monies anymore to do anything. When I get it, I give it to the kids. I don't even look forward to it, because it's hate money! But, hey, we'll spend it. Maybe I'll learn how to invest it!"

Words of Wisdom from Lawyer Myrna Felder

No. 1. WHEN YOUR HUSBAND IS A SICKO, GET OUT! I have lots of clients who will always say to me that the most important thing is that they're divorced from him! This is because there are some things that are more important than money. You have to realize that there are a lot of people who stay in very, very destructive relationships because they are afraid. And that, of course, is the meaning of having your own career—if you know that if you had to, you could make your own living.

I'm always amazed at all the talk about divorce being too easy. My experience has been that people are very reluctant to divorce. And they only get divorced when it's really *horrible*. When you hear what went on, you wonder how people could put up with it. What happens in an abusive situation like Donna's is that a message is being sent every day: "You are stupid, you can't do anything, you need me." It's very hard for anybody to withstand that.

No. 2. DON'T LET ANY MAN CASH YOUR CHECK. You work hard for the money. It is nonnegotiable. If he insists, start shopping for a new mate.

No. 3. BEFORE YOU TELL HIM YOU WANT OUT, RUN, DON'T WALK, TO THE BANK TO WITHDRAW YOUR HALF OF THE MONEY. Get your fair share before he has the chance to beat you to the window and clean out your bank account and you!

No. 4. MONEY IS NOT JUST ABOUT MONEY. It's about control, power, freedom. He used it to control her. She needed it to set herself free.

Linda: 40 years old
Marital status: Divorced, mother of 2 young boys; husband was a
                      pilot

Job: Former flight attendant
Home: Seattle

"His job pays him $100,000.
I'm a wonderful mom, but it pays nothing."

When I worked as a flight attendant, I was very free with money. I didn't bother putting any aside. If I had $10 in the account, I could spend $9 on dinner. My goal was to be married and taken care of.

I kept working when we got married. I made about $30,000 a year and Sandy didn't have a problem with me keeping my play money in my account. That was quite private and quite nice. Then, at some point, we joined our money out of necessity.

Money was not a big deal for me. I never hoarded it. Sandy was raised much differently. His parents divorced in high school. His dad grew up very poor. From Sandy's standpoint, money is power in every sense.

I wrote the checks for our bills, and when I would put them in the envelopes he would stand over me and say: "Now, did you sign them?" He treated me like I was incapable of taking care of something on my own.

When I was five months' pregnant with my son Joey, I stopped working. He's now eight and a half years old. It was awful not making my own money. I certainly had the credit cards and Sandy would pay for things, but he was always looking over my shoulder and questioning me about any purchases I made.

"Oh, the Nordstrom's bills seem to have gotten a little big," he would say. He wouldn't ask whether I needed what I bought or whether the kids needed things. He was just very righteous in any of his opinions. No matter what I said, his tone was condescending and I would have to justify or defend myself. And I'm not good at defending myself. I would stop and think: He is right!

She Saves, He Spends Like a Sailor

I was always berated for going to the grocery store as often as I did. I was never at liberty to spend money. But in the last couple of years, he would say we were broke. Yet when I looked, we had $10,000 in the checking account. I would be as frugal as I could be—I wouldn't even go up to Starbucks and get a coffee and I would still be in trouble when he came home from his trips. My friend, who was also a flight attendant, told me she was on the same trip with Sandy and that he was spending money right and left: buying dinner and drinks for people and had a fancy rental car. She said she could never understand why I always told her I was so broke.

No matter what Sandy said, it was a stigma to him that I didn't work. He felt that what I did wasn't important enough. Yet he said that this was what we had chosen for me to do! He wanted me to go golfing, but we didn't have the money to pay the sitter all day. I stopped battling. It was a no-win situation. If I had to go through a marriage again, I would like to choose to trust a man, and be acknowledged for what I'm doing, raising and nurturing our children.

I felt I had a job and that I should have been better

compensated for it—thank you for doing what you do! As a mom and running a house, I didn't think I needed a secret stash because we'd both agreed that I would stay home to raise the children. I also work within the community. I am an awesome mom, our kids are just terrific, yet there is the constant berating. No compassion or sympathy from him. I said something to him about money. He snapped at me: "Get a job!"

I don't want to be a deceitful person, but the more I hear about it, you have to be! That is where my being naive and trusting was a curse! I think that is hard for me to accept because I like who I am but these dirtbags teach you differently. Our marriage was distant for many years. It took me a while to realize that nothing was getting better. When I said we should go to counseling, he said it wasn't worth it, we couldn't afford it. He was only home one week a month for years of our marriage. That was part of the problem.

HIS CHEATIN' HEART

Last November, I looked through his suitcase and found candles and an empty perfume box, and a jewelry box that obviously had had a ring in it. I felt wretched for looking.

I found his cellular phone bill. I was instantly suspicious because there was one number on it where he spoke for fifteen minutes and he is so damned cheap I wondered who that was. His mom was in the hospital—he was supposed to be with her. And he wasn't. I asked him about that and he said, "If you don't want to know the answer, don't ask me!"

He was having an affair with someone I know! We vacationed together! Melissa, the other woman, had already told her husband that she and Sandy had something going. Her husband knew, but I didn't know anything about it! I liked to have fun with Sandy, but he would tell me I wasn't any fun. I felt so betrayed! A lot of the airline people knew about the affair. At the time, I had $10 in my checking account and he had $10,000 in his. I couldn't have been in a worse position.

I asked Sandy to leave the first of the year. I wanted to overcome something so hurtful. We truly did have a loveless marriage. I didn't want the kids growing up thinking this kind of marriage was all right. He went to counseling twice and quit!

He is not living here but we are not legally separated. Now he pays the bills. He pays for everything for the house and $700 extra, and he gives me $500 for groceries. It's very tight. I am very much at his mercy.

He just bought me a car. He said I could look for something about $15,000! Do you know what you can get these days for $15,000? Not much. It went from bad to worse. He picked it out. The last check he gave me, there was $100 extra! By that he thinks he is being a really big guy. The check he gives me, it doesn't pay for anything extra, like sports stuff for the kids.

When we were talking about arranging this separation, I said to him, "Do you know how hard it will be for me? I will have no retirement, no pension." His answer?

How to Hide Money from Your Husband ...

"You'll get married again!" I said, "I have no intention of doing that now! I don't want to open myself up to the wounds I am suffering now." He said he would take care of me and the boys. But his friend told me, "Sandy will screw you the first chance he gets!"

Sandy doesn't know I have a lawyer. My mom is paying for that. I am not as naive as I'm leading him to believe. Through a lot of this, I never realized I was a victim of his emotional and verbal abuse. I would cower and not fight back!

Words of Wisdom from Lawyer Myrna Felder

No. 1. LEARN YOUR HUSBAND'S MONEY PERSONALITY WHILE YOU'RE DATING. Observe his behavior closely. Ask him leading questions about spending, what he likes to spend on and what he doesn't so you are not surprised, disappointed, or crushed later on. Particularly in this day and age, when women often live with men or have long relationships before they marry, women have a chance to look at their partner's money philosophy. Be *very, very careful* if you see what amounts to a pathology about money because it's only going to get worse once you marry. If this is how somebody is when they are courting you, imagine when they've got you!

No. 2. DISCUSS MONEY WITH YOUR HUSBAND JUST LIKE YOU DISCUSS BIRTH CONTROL—WAY BEFORE YOU WALK DOWN THE AISLE.

No. 3. DON'T LIVE FRUGALLY IF YOU DON'T

HAVE TO! IT WILL ONLY HURT YOU IN THE END!
SPEND! ENJOY! One of the biggest mistakes women
make when there is trouble in their marriage is to cut back
on what they spend. They don't want to make the situation worse. Unfortunately, a woman in Linda's situation,
where the husband has made her spend very little, is in a
very bad position when it comes to seeking maintenance
from the court. Because the court is going to determine
how much support to award her based on what she usually spent before they were separated. The period the
court looks to is one year, two years before. And she has
established a very low standard. That's why women who
are bitchy, who have been extravagant and spent beyond
their husband's means, do great.

No. 4. HE PROBABLY HAS MORE MONEY THAN
SHE THINKS. If Linda went to court she might have to
illustrate how he is living when he is not with her. So this
is a case where witnesses, like the flight attendant who
saw him spending freely on a business trip, could be helpful. She could follow up on some of those leads. When
she goes to the lawyer, she can help the lawyer with information like that. If she can establish what he hid from
her by proving what he was spending on himself, she
might be able to influence the court and get more support.

No. 5. GET PAID A SALARY FOR RAISING KIDS
AND TAKING CARE OF A HOME AND YOUR HUS-
BAND. THERE IS NO BIGGER JOB. If you are a homemaker, your husband can also contribute $2,000 to an IRA
for you every year until retirement age. If you do put your

career on hold for him or to raise your kids, make sure your work in the house and with the children has a dollar value. It would cost a man plenty to hire women to do that for him if you dropped dead and he had to. No reason you shouldn't be paid, too!

Financial Tips for Your Forties and Fifties

- SAVE! SAVE! SAVE!
- Keep contributing to your 401K, or Keogh if you are self-employed.
- Write a will or update the one you have.
- If you decide to hire a financial adviser, first check her or him out carefully. Become informed. Ask questions before you give your money to a stranger.
- Make sure you have enough insurance—life, homeowner, auto, and liability—to make sure your holdings are protected.
- Investigate a long-term-care insurance policy.

4

Men: Their Tricks of the Trade

(And Other Helpful Hints for Women
Who Are Getting or Giving the Boot)

"Would you mind getting lunch? All my money is in a blind trust."

Richard Friedman, forensic accountant, could write a book. If your husband is hiding money that he didn't want to share with you during your marriage and certainly doesn't want to part with come divorce, Friedman can track it down. What makes a case easy or hard depends on how long and how well your husband has been stashing your marital cash. But there is no hiding from Friedman. He does almost a hundred divorce cases a year, representing women most of the time. His advice for women, knowing what he knows?

"Women ought to build a war chest, little by little, even putting money in a box, so if a divorce comes, they have a few bucks to be able to survive."

It is no secret that men historically have been the hiders and deceivers. So the very worst thing a woman can do, says Friedman, is to keep herself in the dark about the family's finances. If divorce does appear on your marital horizon, you and your children could wind up destitute. We're talking survival here.

So how and where do men hide money from their wives? Here are some of the most common places Friedman has discovered they stash it. Check these spots out if you think this is happening to you.

How and Where Do Men Hide Money? Let Me Count the Ways . . .

1. IN A BANK VAULT.
2. IN A SAFE-DEPOSIT BOX AT HOME OR IN THE OFFICE.
3. OVERSEAS. If you can prove that money left the country, get the court to order your husband to provide the documents. Otherwise it's usually too expensive and extremely hard to get the documents from overseas. Favorite countries where men like to stash their cash include: Switzerland, the Bahamas, the Cayman Islands, Luxembourg, and Lichtenstein. They all have bank secrecy laws and protect the privacy of clients' accounts.
4. BY TRANSFERRING MONEY TO A "NOMINEE." For example: A man gives his friend a "gift" of $50,000. The friend opens an account as a favor to his buddy, knowing full well the money is the husband's. At the deposition, the husband pleads the Fifth as to whose money this really is. You and your attorney know immediately that something phony is going on.
5. BY TRANSFERRING MONEY TO AN OFFSHORE TRUST.
6. BY POSTPONING INCOME TO A FUTURE TIME. For example: A man will make a deal with his boss, telling him: "Don't pay me the bonus this month. Wait until after my divorce."

7. BY CREATING LIABILITIES THAT ARE NOT REAL.
This is a common ruse to make your husband look as if he
has less money to divide with you. For example: He claims
he owes someone $30,000 . . . but he really doesn't. It's just
a wink and a nod between him and his collaborating friend
or relative. Remember: The less money or assets he can
make you believe he has, the less he has to share with you.

DALLYING FOR DOLLARS

Another tactic men use to cheat you out of your fair share
of the marital pot is by refusing to hand over the financial
documents needed to get an accurate picture of all marital
assets. Often, the wife will use up all the money she has in
lawyers' or accountants' fees to pursue such documents.
When she begins to run out of money, she feels forced to
settle.

"When the husband has control of everything, more
often than not during the initial stages of the divorce,
the wife is destroyed," explains Friedman, who is both a
lawyer and an accountant. "She gets a small order of support from the judge to keep her head above water. She
has no cash to her name. Suddenly her lifestyle is cut to
nothing. Now she is suffering and these cases don't
move fast. From the date you make a temporary applica-
tion of relief until you get the order of support can be
many months. It is the wife, then, who takes the mental,
psychological, and emotional beating to the point at
which she says she has to settle for much less than she is
entitled to."

Don't Be Such a Smart Shopper:
Bargain Hunters Often Finish Last!

132

It might also be a good idea to start spending a little more in the years before the divorce if you think divorce is coming your way. Adjust your pattern. Try to save your receipts. But since that can be a burden, and your husband is likely to find the big box of receipts and chuck it, Friedman says, the courts will be just as happy if you keep a notebook for ten years in which you write down your purchases and, on average, what they have cost.

If you know you are sticking it out with an awful man until your kids are grown, "try to set your style of life up so that when and if you get divorced, you can maintain the style of life you'd like to have after the divorce." (Of course the fallacy with this is that two don't live as well as one when there are two households to support.) The money may not be there to support the pre-separation style of life. But the statute presumes that the money is there. Similarly, experts advise you not to hoard your separation agreement maintenance money by sticking it in the bank. (That's the money the court awards you to support yourself while the divorce case is wending its way through the system.) If you do, the judge may think you don't actually need the full amount he awarded you and will end up cutting your alimony.

In order to avoid that happening to you, SPEND CONSISTENT WITH WHAT YOU HAVE ALWAYS SPENT TO LIVE. FIGHT THE FEAR AND USE THE

MONEY! And again, save all your receipts. Documents are everything in divorce today.

Seek and You Shall Find—Tracking Down His Ass(ets)

How does Friedman track down marital money that is legally yours but that your husband wants to hoard for himself? Here is his checklist:

1. Look at his income and assets. The biggest assets in the United States are the family home and the pension account. Once you get beyond that, you've generally eliminated 85 percent of the resources at stake. A good attorney should be able to look very quickly at you and your husband's entire financial picture and tell you, within reason, what's going to be the end result of the case. Luckily, today most financial transactions are traceable.

2. The first giveaway is a tax return. (SEE THE FORM IN THE BACK OF THE BOOK TO SEND AWAY FOR A COPY OF YOUR JOINT RETURN.) Look at the man's lifestyle, his spending history and patterns. The tax return may say he earned $50,000 but he could be living on $500,000. I also look at his checking accounts, credit card statements, and brokerage accounts.

3. The easier cases involve higher paid, high-earning husbands. Take O. J. Simpson, for example. Hertz didn't pay him with a briefcase full of cash. He got a check, then a 1099 tax form at the end of the year. His income was reported to the government. Those are not easy things to

hide. What Friedman does is to follow transactions: If your husband thinks he's being cute by writing $2,000 checks each month to his mother to put in a piggy bank for him so you can't get to it, he will be sorely surprised when your lawyer and accountant trace those checks to Mom's bank account. There are paper trails, electronic or otherwise, that track virtually every monetary transaction we make.

(Make sure you write down every one of your husband's bank and brokerage account numbers. This will save you a lot of money in lawyer's fees and your lawyer a lot of time not having to search for this crucial information.)

4. Hunting down how much money a deceitful spouse has gets hard when men own their own business. One has to ascertain the value of the business and the real income the husband enjoys. A W-2 tax form may say his yearly income is $150,000, but it doesn't cover perks: cars, entertainment, travel, which all get written off for the company.

5. One of the oldest tricks men use is to get the financial value of their business down. This is divorce poverty syndrome, or as one attorney coined the phrase: RAIDS—"Recently Acquired Income Deficiency Syndrome." When this happens, the wife must hire a business evaluator to come in. This is nearly impossible to do on a privately held company. And it could cost a fortune in fees.

    "The one case I refuse to handle is the owner of the candy store," Friedman says. "He buys for cash, sells for cash. Everything is cash. So there is no easy way to trace the money."

6. Once a husband's income is blocked out, Friedman looks at their lifestyle. He looks at checkbooks, credit card re-

ceipts, the kind of house a family has, the real estate taxes they are paying, the mortgage. From this he learns the estimated disposable income of the family. Then he can match that amount with the reportable income.

Next, he interviews the wife. How often does she go to the gym? What does she spend on clothes, cosmetics, health care, health club, you name it. Most times it is the wife who is the lesser earner, but not always.

For example, in the Elizabeth Taylor/Larry Fortensky split, the reverse was true. The couple had been married for six and a half years and the only money he had was the money she gave him. So Mr. Fortensky had to sit down and write out his budget. Since California is a "community property," or "fifty-fifty," state, he got half of what she earned in those six and a half years they were married. Not bad!

7. Digging to find the truth can be expensive. Friedman describes one case in which it cost the wife $300,000 to pinpoint exactly what her husband had, but he found millions by going through his tax return and all of his accounts! They caught him writing checks to himself for $50,000. He called that "pocket money."

Luckily, says Friedman, in this modern electronic age, unless you are carrying briefcases full of money out of the country, you cannot hide it easily. It is true, however, that if you have a husband who wants to protect himself, he can do so quietly, without anyone noticing over the years, to the point where he has amassed a small fortune. How? Each year, he moves 10 or 15 percent of the marital estate to where you will never find it. He does this by cashing a check for $500 each month for ten years. You think it's just his spending money. (This technique, of course, is available to women, too.)

8. If you are married to a rich man, beware of stocks that bear no dividends! You don't have to report your stock holdings on your income tax form if they don't pay any dividends. A crafty guy might have a portfolio of non-dividend-paying stocks for just that reason. They stay hidden from you!

Friedman's Friendly Advice—We'd Be Crazy Not to Follow It

No. 1. Any wife who thinks she has a shaky marriage should start keeping a record of what she spends, and perhaps spend a little more, without looking ridiculous.

No. 2. Stop hiding your head in the sand and realize that even though you may not have handled the family finances, you are capable of doing so and you should not be intimidated by money! What you don't know can and will hurt you. If you play ostrich for ten to fifteen years and then your marriage falls apart, you will be in big trouble if you then try for the first time to determine what your family finances were. The women who get hurt the most are those who have had no interest in their finances.

No. 3. Even if you have a good marriage, there's no reason why one spouse should control all the money. And remember: It's too late to make this an issue when the marriage starts falling apart.

No. 4. Put some assets in your name only. Get stocks in your own name—a gift to yourself. Put some money aside for yourself that is just yours and keep it private. Do not let it be touched.

No 5. A wife should know when to sue. Very important! For example: A wife is very unhappy and she wants out in the worst possible way. She runs off half-cocked to a lawyer who then runs to court to file a summons and a complaint. The husband is served the divorce papers and he has a smile from ear to ear! Why?

137

Because he knows that in six months, on his tenth anniversary with the company, he becomes qualified for thousands and thousands of dollars' worth of stock options or is getting a huge promotion. Advice: Bite your tongue to the extent possible and wait until he passes his tenth anniversary.

No. 6. A few words about your nest egg! Whether you secretly open a bank or a money market account with a mature child, a relative, or a friend, have something put away in case of an emergency. If you can, be honest and stand up for your own rights. Tell your husband: "I'm taking $10,000 out of our account and putting it into an account with my name only on it. That way, if something happens to you, if you drop dead, the children and I are not going to starve while we wait to go through probate." Ladies—stand up to your husband and say this is what has to be!

Read This and Weep

If Friedman's advice makes you uncomfortable, if you think you don't have the stomach to look out for yourself in this way, maybe you will change your mind after reading the following material. Men already have a book to tell them everything they have to do to rob you blind. Here's an example of how divorce lawyer Timothy J. Horgan arms men in his book *Winning Your Divorce—A Man's Survival Guide* (New York: Plume/Penguin, 1995).

Are you sitting down?

1. "Go to the bank immediately and close both your joint checking and savings accounts."

2. "If your spouse has joint access to safe-deposit boxes, remove the contents before she does. Typically, people keep cash, stocks, bonds and jewelry—all very liquid assets—in a safe deposit box." [Ladies, remember Myrna Felder's advice—you can get a restraining order to stop this.]

3. "Lower your standard of living. Determine whether you have been unduly generous with your wife and family. . . . Try to do everything in your power to reduce your wife's personal spending lest you be forced to continue paying [your wife's] bills after your divorce. Talk down your income, moan about your expenses, but do everything possible to lower your standard of living."

4. "You should collect all your family's financial documents—tax returns, bank statements, deeds, wills and such—so that your lawyer will have the necessary information. More important, your wife and her attorney must now face the preliminary obstacle of estimating your financial worth and the true extent of your marital property, without ready access to your papers. If your wife was the type of individual who was uninterested in the family financial status, don't start educating her now by leaving a paper trail!"

138

5. "Encourage your wife to seek work. The better her job, the more likely her pleas for support will fall on [a judge's] deaf ears."

On the subject of fighting for custody of your children, Horgan tells men, "Always ask for custody. . . . Local courts look favorably upon fathers who seek custody of their children." Yet in the next breath he says it may be better for dating new women if you don't have your kids living with you. (Besides cramping his dating style, all that parental responsibility would be like taking an ice cold shower. It is only the rarest of men who are actually in the day-to-day trenches of child care and all the responsibility and obligation that entails.)

"Another factor to consider in deciding whether to try to gain custody [of your children] is that you will be starting a new life," he writes. "You will become more socially involved than in the past and you will begin dating again. For this reason, it might be in your best interests to see the kids on weekends, rather than having them live with you."

So this is how the guys talk.

Have you had enough, ladies? Are you mad yet? Ready to even the score? Horgan's book should make any woman's blood boil. But remember the words of Godfather Michael Corleone: "Keep your friends close, your enemies closer." Well, you've met the enemy. He is the one who doesn't pick up his dirty socks every night.

Remember: Divorce *is* war and you must have a battle plan and money in the bank to finance it.

Making matters worse for women in many places in this country is the fact that divorce judges often come from the bottom of the judicial barrel. Although things are changing, there are still plenty of sexist jurists sitting up there who are not going to do you any favors. Cases can also take forever to make their way through the system.

These factors are all the more reason women need a nest egg to win their freedom and sanity. The amount of money needed to fight can be enormous. Women are the losers if they can't level the financial playing field.

Other Considerations

Togetherness, But Not in the Slammer! Think Before You Sign a Joint Tax Return

DID YOU KNOW . . . that if your dearly beloved is trying to hide income from the government, is avoiding paying taxes, or is in some kind of disreputable financial dealings, THE IRS CAN HOLD YOU RESPONSIBLE FOR HIS DEBTS? AND YOU CAN BE WIPED OUT OF EVERY PENNY YOU HAVE IN A HEARTBEAT?

You sure can. Be aware of what you are signing when you sign a joint tax return. In some marriages, you must avoid getting stuck with your husband's liabilities.

The reason people file jointly, of course, is because the tax rate is better and there is a monetary saving. Most women tell their husbands, "Fine, I'll sign." But, warns matrimonial attorney Myrna Felder, if there is trouble in paradise, or if you are at all concerned that your husband may be a little bit or a lot of a crook, you don't want your name on that joint tax return. You can be held liable for all of the taxes—his and yours.

141

WHAT ELSE DO YOU NEED TO KNOW?

In marriages where the husband is the breadwinner and controls every dollar, how does a housewife pay for her own lawyer? Is your husband obligated to pay for the *best* lawyer money can buy, or just your garden-variety matrimonial lawyer?

This, says Myrna Felder, is one of the biggest problems facing women without a nest egg or money of their own. A dependent spouse can have her attorney go to court at the beginning of a divorce case and ask for temporary counsel fees, as well as an appraiser and temporary support, if the husband has cut off the wife from money altogether or has lowered her allowance. The court award should provide for equality in representation, so if a husband hires Edward Bennett Williams or Johnnie Cochran, a judge should be asked for sufficient funds to enable a wife to get a comparable lawyer.

Your husband can also prevent you from getting the best lawyer money can buy by trying to hire those lawyers for himself. If one spouse meets with an attorney for just an hour's consultation, and that lawyer hears the basic facts and finances of your case, that lawyer can no longer represent the other spouse, even if the original spouse decides not to hire that lawyer. So, if a man wants to be cute and vindictive, he will have an hour's consultation with each of the good lawyers in town to prevent them from being hired by you! If you live in a small town with just one or two expert divorce lawyers, your husband could get to them first and make sure you are left with mediocre representation.

The big problem, however, is that most lawyers want to receive a retainer up front, before they start the real work of your divorce. This is a great problem for women without means and can prevent them from getting the same of kind of lawyer their husband has. In cases where neither spouse can afford high costs, many couples try the mediation route. If much of your marital estate is going to be eaten up by lawyers, that's no fun.

GET THEE TO AN ATTORNEY EVEN IF YOU NEVER FILE FOR DIVORCE—KNOW YOUR RIGHTS

Women should seek out a matrimonial lawyer the moment it occurs to them that there is trouble in their marriage. Going for consultation early on is a very good move. It may be years, or never at all, that you file for divorce, but this way you know your rights and what to expect. By conferring with a lawyer early on, you can manage your affairs in the best possible position.

A reminder: Don't pay the matrimonial lawyer with a credit card or a check for a consultation. Pay with cash. There's no sense in alarming or arousing suspicion in your husband so early in the game. You don't want your husband to think that war has been declared . . . yet.

"Sometimes I have heard people say, 'Unless I'm going

to do well financially I don't want to end this marriage,'"
says Felder. "I look at their finances and tell them if they'd
be better off financially to stay in the marriage."

143

How do you know you have picked the right lawyer
for you?

Experts agree that having an easy rapport with your
lawyer is one indicator. Your attorney should make you
feel comfortable, that no question is too stupid or too
foolish to ask. A trap that many women fall into, partly
because they are often so upset, is not understanding
what their lawyer is saying.

It may be a good idea to bring a close friend or a relative along when you go to meet with your attorney. This
can be very helpful because women are, understandably,
often traumatized and in a daze when they finally work up
the emotional fortitude to divorce a man and seek counsel. Visiting a divorce lawyer for the first time is not unlike
going to a big medical appointment that has you anxious
and scared. You may hear every word that is being said,
but you are absorbing nothing because you are so nervous. Felder advises women to choose a lawyer who will
work with you, not the kind who says, "Don't worry your
pretty little head. I will take care of everything."

"Battering in a marriage could just as easily be emotional, not physical, where a woman is beaten down and
has no self-esteem left," she adds. "When you have the
kind of lawyer who just takes over, the lawyer becomes
another controlling person in a woman's life who is really
saying to you, 'I know everything, you know nothing.'
And where have they heard that song before?

"One of the most beautiful things I've experienced as a lawyer is when we walk through the litigation together and women see that they can do it. It is very empowering for them. Women have far greater inner resources than they think. My message is: Have the courage to tap into that!"

Divorce—You Don't Die from It, So Hang in There

One woman who discovered her inner strength through divorce is Susan. Listen to her story:

Susan:	42 years old
Marital status:	Married 13 years, separated; when married she was 22, her husband was 41
Job:	Stockbroker
Home:	San Diego
$$ Strategy:	Initially, none. When the marriage started to deteriorate, a nest egg.

I got married three weeks out of college. It was June 1977. We met here in San Diego at a convention for my sorority. We had a long-distance romance for a year. He was really good-looking. He had a big ego and had done whatever he wanted his whole life.

For the first two years I didn't work. He was in business for himself—in farming. I did the payroll sometimes. Then I took over running our office. Once we got married, my husband didn't want me to work for anyone. He controlled which job I could have and told me I would work for him or not at all. He wanted me to have my time free for him and me. That was a bit of a problem!

I didn't notice at the time we were married that he was a controlling person. But as time went on, it became very clear. I was working for him all the time. He controlled my salary. To keep our taxes down, he kept my salary down. My gross income was $17,000 or $18,000. I would say to him: "Just give me a raise, make me feel like what other clerical workers in the office are making!" But he never did.

SURVIVAL SKILLS

As the marriage started to disintegrate, I got a little smarter. I went and established a credit card in my name. Then I got an American Express card in my own name. He didn't know! I got a few other department store credit cards in my own name as well. I was thirty! We had no kids. He had kids from another marriage.

I'd get so that each paycheck I would cash $100, and I just started rat-holing cash in my nylons drawer in a fake nylons box. We had some marital problems. I think it was then that I opened a checking account of my own. So he didn't know how much there was in the checkbook. I would write down that I had made out a check for $200, but it really was for only $100.

Even if I wrote down that I'd deposited a check for $700, I really deposited only $300 and put the rest into my own checking account. The other great way to stash money was writing the grocery checks for an extra $50 or $100. Put that in your little nest egg! Those were the two easiest ways. The best advice I can give is to keep copies of tax returns, save credit card receipts, save everything! Once I knew I was going to leave, I went out and bought a lot of stuff—stupid stuff like Lancôme makeup, things that would get me through the next six months.

It was almost thirteen years before we separated in 1989. I remember I bought a new comforter and dust ruffle for the bed. My mom was coming to visit. It was $500 and he had a total fit because it was related to my mom. I felt myself filling with hate and venom for him. He could make you feel so small, like you were a child. He would explode over something ridiculous, trying to control me in every way he could. Then I would have to be the peacemaker, the conciliator. That's how the dynamic worked.

When I finally told him that I was going to leave him, that I'd had enough, he was absolutely shocked. He'd had some affairs and we were trying to work it out. He said that it was my fault. His rationale was that I was the traitor because I copied *our* tax returns. Can you believe that?

But I was fearful that he was hiding money. I knew he hid assets from his wife in his prior divorce. He admitted it to me! He was proud of it. He sold some property, dummied her signature on a deed, hid income, manipulated balance sheets. She had no access to any of the tax returns. So I was paranoid. For women to think their husbands will do the right thing by them is so naive! When I worked in the office, I would just start digging.

MY NEST EGG MADE ALL THE DIFFERENCE

I probably had $7,000 in my nest egg when I decided to leave. I needed money for an attorney. I knew I would be completely intimidated by my husband, so I needed a hired gun. The key to my divorce was to hide. Otherwise he would have crushed me. What saved me a lot of money was that I did my own discovery. I photocopied everything! I did it all!

My advice? Women should absolutely have a nest egg. When it comes down to it, you have to be able to take care of yourself and money is the key! You have to forget that Prince Charming syndrome where he takes care of you for the rest of your life! You have to take care of yourself. You need a year's worth of living expenses to at least cover your mortgage and car payment, and always keep it.

After my divorce, I had to buck up and get a job. I went back to school to get my MBA. After two weeks I quit. Fortunately I had some spousal support to give me time to find my niche. I now have a securities license and I'm a stockbroker—managing money for individuals and companies. What I'm doing now I absolutely love. You muddle through the hard times and fall into something. Divorce was not the end of my life, but the beginning.

5

Knowing the Score

The Golden Years

"I'm survived by my wife and eighteen million dollars."

If *you think the battle over money is over because* your youth is, think again! As long as there is a man in your house, the tug of war is on. If you have never been interested in your finances, it is still not too late to learn. In fact, you better.

Until the discrepancy between men's longevity and ours is solved—almost ten years these days—we must plan on living on our own for many years of our lives. And studies by the National Institute on Aging show that when women lose their mates, they are more likely to wind up financially impoverished and in a nursing home. The heck with that! Don't wait until you are eighty to learn how to write a check or balance a checkbook or pay the rent. If your husband is ill, make sure he tells you—if you don't already know—where your bank accounts, mortgage papers, and any other important financial documents are that you may have thought were too boring to look at over the years.

Listen closely to the women in this chapter. They have been in the trenches of marriage, on the money battlefields with men for forty and fifty years, and some press on very inventively after their husbands' deaths. There are stories of love, of grudges well honed, of marriage in all its amazing facets.

Maxine, eighty-three, has been hiding money in her "Jesus box" since the 1940s. Irene, seventy-seven, was widowed at forty-eight, left with two sons still living at home. In the early years of her marriage she was smart enough to build a nest egg, but when her husband's business got into trouble she happily gave it all away to him to start over. Unfortunately, he was a bad businessman and squandered the family's security, which she had so meticulously built up. She has fiercely regretted giving up her nest egg every day of her life. Since her husband's traumatic and unexpected death at a Plaza Hotel wedding, she has been nothing if not up front with the men in her life: "If you want to see me, it will cost you," the newly widowed woman told her married boyfriend. He supported her for twenty-five years.

Catherine, seventy-two, has a husband from the old school. The Des Moines grandmother only wanted a checking account of her own to buy gifts she didn't want to discuss with her husband. He wouldn't hear of it. So in her sixties she did it anyway—opened a secret checking account with her daughter. It has all of $1,000 in it and that's all she needs. Judy, a university professor and author who grew up poor, was a wife and mother until she got her Ph.D. at fifty and bought herself a Cadillac at sixty-five with her nest egg just to drive the twelve blocks to campus!

Most extraordinary of all is Rose Gingold. Living under the financial and emotional tyranny of a controlling and mean-spirited husband, she created a new identity for herself since her husband did everything in his power to rob her of hers. She gave herself the new name of Rose Miller, applied for and got a social security number, and then secretly worked part-time to earn her own money— and squirrel it away for a rainy day. While it was legally questionable to have two identities (though each Rose paid taxes), she is an amazing example of the creative lengths a woman with her back against the wall can go to, to fight back.

Sylvia: 67 years old
Marital status: Divorced once, married to her second husband, Sol, for 27 years; 2 children, 3 grandchildren
Job: Homemaker and part-time manager of clothing boutique; clerical worker at Queens College, Flushing, NY
Home: New York City
$$ Strategy: Skim! Skim! Skim!

"I'm very good at this! From a dollar, I make three.
From three I make five. It doesn't have to be a lot of money.
And it helps a family."

When I was working, I made it a point to have a little nest egg—in case anything happened, God forbid. I'd skim a little something off the top of my paycheck and put it away. My technique for hiding money was simple: I used to keep it in a mug on a shelf. And Sol was unaware. Sometimes he would say to me, "Are you putting money away?" And I would say, "Bothers you? Whenever we need something, it's here, Sol. It's for both of us." And I wasn't hoarding. One time when I was working, we had a state tax problem. Suddenly, we owed the state $1,000, which was a lot of money for us. And I paid it back to the IRS all at one time! It came right out of my mug. I never put it in the bank. I wanted it to be there whenever I needed it.

154

The most I ever had in the mug was, would you believe, $10,000. Oh, I'm very good at this! From a dollar, I make three. From three, I make five! It doesn't have to be a lot of money. And it helps my family. My son has been unemployed, and who's going to help him? A mother, that's who. If my daughter ever needed me, I would help her, too.

Sol is my second husband and I was insecure when I married him. He made me laugh. He was very funny. But he's not funny now. He's an old crab apple. He drives a car service a few days a week and when he comes home he has nothing to say. Now that he's older, he's better with money. But in the beginning, he had full control. He'd dole it out to me and I couldn't stand it. Every time I looked at him, I wanted to kill him. He would go shopping with me for food just to watch how much I'd spend. I hated that. I guess he thought I would fly away with the money! He had no trust.

YOU CAN TEACH AN OLD DOG NEW TRICKS

Now he gives me $60 a day. Every night, he would put that money on my dresser, and I'd say: "What do you think I am, a prostitute? Why can't you put it in my hand?" We'd laugh, because this money was for the house. And he gives me a $300-a-week allowance, for food, detergent, and all the things you need to run a house. He has congestive heart failure, so he doesn't eat beef anymore, which is a savings. He used to eat beef every day, but now he eats turkey and chicken. No rib steaks, no skirt steaks.

I'd have to say that since he's gotten sick, and now that he's older, there's a great improvement in the way we handle money. Now he doesn't say anything when I shop. And we went for counseling on money issues. The counselor made me realize that he's a control freak, but that he has low self-esteem. He doesn't need a new shirt, or new pants. Just give him his food and things like that. A clean bed. If there was garbage on the floor, he'd walk over it.

It gets to the point where if I buy him some pants, a new shirt, he will holler, "Who am I? Frank Sinatra?" He doesn't think he's worthy of this! He says, "Why does it have to be a shopping spree?"

I've never had this kind of marriage before. It was one pot of money before, and this has been a new experience in my life. And why do men want all this power, this control? Who knows? I guess it goes back to the caveman. To tell you the truth, I used to resent him terribly.

But my husband can also be good-natured. Whenever we have an anniversary, there's always a card and flowers. He gets theater tickets; he's thoughtful that way. But he was a bad money manager, and I did a much better job. He would spend all his money like a drunken sailor, and then get angry with me when I challenged him.

I'd get a set of beautiful earrings, a bracelet or a gold

heart, and I would say, "It's beautiful." Then I would holler—"I'm gonna kill you for spending all that money when we have bills to pay!" We always fought over money. That's life. That's marriage. What are you going to do?

Life Lessons from Sylvia

1. Women need to find ways to put money aside, especially older women, who, like me, come from a generation where they feel they've been done out of something by men. They need to have their own nest egg. Financial independence is essential to a happy life.

2. Men might be control freaks, but women are often much better at handling money in a household. Don't be intimidated by your husband and his power trips. Be strong, stand your ground. If necessary, seek out counseling on money issues. It can only strengthen your marriage.

3. When it comes to hiding money, a man is bolder than a woman. They do it without blinking an eye. Women worry: "Should I, shouldn't I?" I told this to my daughter years ago. She used to have a little job in addition to raising the children. She'd say, "I paid this bill, I paid that bill." And I'd say, "What are you, stupid? What does *he* pay? Bev, stop paying those bills! Put the money away for yourself and the kids or for a rainy day."

4. Does she want to put some money into the house? Fine! But skim a little for yourself, I tell her. Make a *knipple.* Have a little bit for yourself. It's very important. If you see something nice and you really want it and can't afford it, you have your little *knipple* and you buy yourself a present.

And Other Time-Honored Ways to Build a Nest Egg

Everybody deserves a present—especially if you are kicking in and working, too.

5. And what if you want him to buy something new for the house—new banisters or a new kitchen and he doesn't want to give it to you? The heck with him and his money! His money is going to be your money anyway when he drops dead. Buy whatever you want yourself, with your own money. You'll get the pleasure of the new banisters or kitchen or whatever and the hell with him! You only live once, so why deny yourself waiting for a tightwad or a control freak to tell you when you can or can't have what you want.

Irene:	77 years old
Marital status:	Widowed mother of 2 when she was 48 (husband, Irving, died at 52); lovers: Adolph and Joe
Job:	Homemaker
Home:	Boca Raton, Florida, and Manhattan
$$ Strategy:	Squirrel, squirrel, squirrel

"Men are funny—they're here today but gone tomorrow.
As a woman, you should save your own money
and not even discuss it."

Don't ever give your nest egg up! Get a man to pay and put the money away! I was married at twenty-three. My husband was in the textile business with his uncle. This was 1943, during World War II, and we were doing very well in those days in the ladies' undergarment business, making slips. My husband was pulling in a lot of money. He wound up taking over the business and running mills in Rhode Island—250 looms that worked three shifts around the clock.

We lived very comfortably on East 88th Street between Madison and Fifth avenues. It was a huge apartment, a two-bedroom, three-bath affair, and the rent was $150 a month! In those days, $150 was a lot of money. Up to that point I had worked for the National Silver Company as a junior executive, making $35 a week. I had graduated from New York University with a bachelor's degree in merchandising and business administration. My first job was at Lord & Taylor, for $18 a week.

When they didn't make me president of the company after two months, I said, "This isn't for me." So I went to a placement bureau and got the job with National Silver. I loved the excitement of business and worked there a year. But when I got married, I stopped working. And two years later I had Charles, the first of my two sons. Life was good.

We had a nurse when he was born, along with a housekeeper and a maid. My husband was paying all the bills, and he gave me an allowance of $1,500 a month! I could do whatever I wanted with the money. If I wanted clothes, he paid the charges. He bought me cars and we had one of the first television sets. Money came so fast and we were so young. There were just no restrictions.

THE NEST EGG IS SACRED

I put the $1,500 a month I got into a checking account, and if I didn't spend it, I put it into a savings account—a nest egg because I was used to saving. I just knew to do that. My mother taught me. My mother also used to tell me that whatever is yours is your husband's. She never told me to hide anything. So when my husband needed the money, I gave my nest egg to him. But I shouldn't have done that. This money should have been for myself and my children. More on that in a minute.

We had five incredible years financially. But after the war, we were suddenly left destitute. Our business fortunes changed. We had been so affluent, but when my husband's business began declining I gave him the money I had been saving. I must have given him close to $400,000. After all, it's your husband. You want to help him. When my husband needed $7,500 for the payroll, I went to the bank and took it out. I was running to the bank every day to get him money. The man at the bank kept asking me, "Are you sure you have to take out this money?" I cashed in the jewelry I had purchased, and that was a big mistake. I hocked two diamond rings, a nine-carat diamond necklace, a pin, all for the paltry sum of $3,000. I cashed in bonds that were given to my children when they were born. I depleted everything we had for his next business ventures, which were all pretty much failures. That is my biggest regret. Once you save something, you should keep it! I knew all the time that I might be making a mistake, saying to my-self, "Don't throw good money after bad." But he kept say-ing to me, "What do *you* know?" He wanted to go into a supermarket business next, another expedition—and I gave him money for that. That business didn't last long ei-ther. Maybe a year or two.

In 1958, I went back to work. I let the maid go. I let the nurse go. There was no money. I went to find work at Bergdorf's and at Bendel's, and they all wanted me, but wanted to pay me nothing. I think Bergdorf's was offering $55 a week! It was just awful. He couldn't get a job. He only wanted to be a boss. He was very immature.

My husband had a series of financial "reverses," and then at the age of fifty-two, he died suddenly. We were at a wedding at the Plaza Hotel. He put his head on my shoulder—I thought to tell me that he was tired. But when I looked down, he was out cold. The paramedics came but he was dead on arrival at the hospital. It was 1969. I was forty-eight, my sons were nineteen and twenty-two, and I was supporting them. My parents had to help me. I still had to put my sons through college and graduate school. And my nest egg had dwindled to nothing! When my husband died, I had no credit cards. The sheriff was at the door. It was a terrible time in my life. My husband turned out to be a terrible businessman. On top of that, he didn't pay his taxes. I found papers after he died saying that he, *we*, owed the government $100,921 in back taxes!

FROM BACK TAXES TO BIG BUCKS

Luckily, I was working for a dentist at the time, and a patient who worked for Sterling Bank told me to borrow some money. He said that was the only way you could get credit. I used that borrowed money to take a stab at getting into the stock market, and bought 100 shares of pub-

lic utilities for $1,900. I sold it not long ago for $18,000! It
was my first investment.

A year or two before my first husband died, I met
Adolph at a country club. He had always had an eye for
me, and when my husband passed away he paid a condo-
lence call. He kept calling me for lunch and dinner and I
kept saying no. Finally I said yes, and we became fast
friends. It led to other things. He came over for drinks
one night, and when I served shrimp to him he asked,
"How do you do it on your budget?" I said, "It's not easy.
My mother is helping me. I'm working hard to put food
on the table, but this is very hard. So, if you want me to
see you exclusively, you'll have to help me financially."

He wound up supporting me for twenty-five years. I
was his other wife.

Now, Adolph was in a bad marriage. Everyone knew.
He went his own way. His wife didn't want to give him a
divorce, and so I saw him Wednesdays, Saturdays, and
Sundays. He paid my rent, which was $400 a month, my
telephone, my electric. When the building went co-op in
1973 I was able to buy my apartment. I drew on the
$30,000 my father had left me. But as I said, Adolph paid
all my bills. He used to bitch if I spent $22 on him for a
sweater. I got Social Security at sixty-two and I was still
working. I would tell him I didn't have money for this or
that and he would pay for things. I didn't buy many
clothes. I was able to, but I saved the money instead.

Meanwhile, I had backed into a nice little jewelry
business. I would buy copies of Cartier and Rolex watches
and did a nice cash business. I'd buy them for $20 to $30

apiece, and sell them for $75. I'd get calls from customers in Cleveland, Ohio, from IBM, everywhere. And Adolph knew nothing about this! Or if he knew, he didn't want to know. I was designing bead necklaces. I told him, "If I had $1,000 I could build up a nice business." He didn't want to give me the money, but I wound up doing it anyway.

We had a great relationship, I loved him. We traveled all over the world together—to Europe, India, and Iran— and that was the big bonus. He was a very prominent and intelligent architect who did Saks Fifth Avenue stores and malls in Europe.

YOUR MONEY, MY VAULT

There came a time when we talked about finances and the future. What inspired the conversation was that he needed a heart bypass operation. He went to the Mayo Clinic and I went with him. He had several operations, and we began talking about what would happen if something happened to him. "What is going to happen to me?" I asked. He said, "Don't worry!" He said he would put me in his will, but when I said I wanted to see the will, it turned out I was in for $50,000. I said, "That's not enough!" So he put me in for $75,000! Later he took the extra money out and gave me all this b.s. that he didn't want his sons to know about me and so he took me out of his will. He said he had $50,000 in stocks in his vault, and he would leave those to me, and I said, "*Your* vault? What's wrong with *my* vault?"

I made a big fuss and so one day he took me to the vault and gave me the stocks to put in my own safe-deposit box. When he died that was all I got from him. If I hadn't made him go do that, there would have been nothing for me. For twenty-five years, I was really a wife to him. I truly loved him. I provided him with companionship, love, affection. I took care of him when he was sick. I cooked for him. We went dancing every Saturday night. I felt entitled to the perks of a wife.

163

Adolph died in 1993, and by that time I'd squirreled away $100,000 of my own from my own stuff and from money he gave me to live on. And it wasn't really stealing. Let's say your husband gives you $50 a week for food. I only spent $30. What was I going to do—go over to him and announce that I had $20 left over? No! You put it away and save it! He gave me $90 a week spending money. And I didn't spend it. It went right in the bank. I'd give him my bills to pay—my rent, credit cards, electric bill. He did it although he always complained.

If we went out or traveled, it was always the best, first class. He didn't care what he spent as long as he was participating. If it was just for me, then he would grumble. He liked calling the shots.

So I'm a big believer in the nest egg. It gives you independence and security. And that means survival. I don't think you can rely on anyone but yourself. You can't rely on someone else's good nature when you're down and out. You have to do these things yourself.

ONCE, TWICE, THREE TIMES A LADY

The man I'm going with now, Joe, would love me to be totally dependent on him. We were in a drugstore the other
day and I picked up a $1 Hershey bar and he said, "I'm not
paying for that! You don't need it!" That's control for you!
Men want control.

It's an entirely new world these days. Today, a man
tells a woman what her half of the check is! With the man
I'm with now, I don't pay for anything but my rent. He
buys the clothes. He pays for everything in Florida. I have
a series of massages, beauty parlor appointments. And this
is what I'm used to. It makes for a better relationship. If
you can get it from a man, that's great!

But you do pay a price. You lose your own self. I'm
kind of submissive; many times I want to explode, but I
don't. You give up a certain amount of independence. He
doesn't drive a car; I'm the driver. And I want to go to the
club, to the doctor. But the priority is what he wants to
do. So I'm captive in that respect because he pays for
everything.

Look, everybody's got their own *mishegoss*.

I am still saving money. Joe is very generous. He buys
me clothes, he likes to spend $75 every night on dinner.
Which I think is a waste, but he likes to do it. To tell you
the truth, I enjoy the time we live together in Florida but
I prefer it when I'm on my own back in New York, in my
own apartment—he has his own apartment—and I can
come and go as I please. I now have enough security, I can
live very well financially with or without a man.

Life Lessons from Irene

1. I think the big mistake women make, if they do have a nest egg, is to give it up without a lot of thought. You are better off sometimes keeping it to support your husband and family than gambling it away on his business. This is something that is not often said, but I think every woman should be independent and have her own money. When my husband needed the money, I gave it to him, but I shouldn't have done that. *Nobody's going to worry about you but you!*

2. You pay a big price for depending on a man's financial support; you lose a lot of your independence and your voice. You live according to his wishes, not yours.

3. Some men encourage independence, and some do not. But women should have their own little bank account so they don't have to come to a man and hassle him for every little thing. Maybe it should be spelled out before you get married.

4. Be strong no matter what happens in your life.

Maxine:	83 years old
Marital status:	Widowed at 28 when her husband John was killed in World War II. The couple had an 18-month-old daughter at the time. Remarried to Harlan, a retired veterinarian. Mother of 2 and grandmother of 2.
Job:	Nurse, homemaker
Home:	Ferndale, California
$$ Strategy:	Jesus box

"I started hiding money in the 1940s . . . It's a little nicer if you have something secret. Just a little hiding place.

165

*Once in a while I'll send a friend who is a missionary
in Africa a little bit. And there is no discussing it
with anyone. No arguments with a man about this.
I just do what I want to. And that feels good."*

I started hiding money in the 1940s. If the kids need
something for an emergency, I use it for that. And I've
always given to the church with money that I earned
myself. This all started because I was married once before.

My first husband was killed in the service, in Oki-
nawa, and I got a small insurance policy from him. It
started at $40 a month and went up to $70. I went out and
got a small cigar box, a beautiful wooden box, and I
Scotch-taped a picture of Jesus on it. The side of it has
sayings from Scriptures, and I call it my "Jesus box."

Once, my daughter came to me with her boyfriend
and said he needed some money. Wendy showed him the
cigar box, and he told me later that he'd borrowed some
money and left a check in there. I said, "I sure hope you
didn't make it out to Jesus!" I've got about $500 in it right
now, and I've been putting that $70 a month from the in-
surance policy in there for fifty years.

SAVE A DOLLAR—GIVE A DOLLAR

I give money every Sunday to the church, about a tenth
of what I have every month. But my husband pays no attention. He knows the cigar box is my church box, but I
don't think he knows I have money in the box.

Last month, I bought a new computer and took a class on the Internet. So why, you might ask, did I start doing this years ago? I just wanted to have money of my own that wasn't HIS! I'd always been sort of independent. I grew up in San Jose, California. There were eight of us, as well as my parents, and we all went through the Depression. My parents saved every cent they could. It was my parents' wish that all the kids go to college, which we all did. We just took it for granted that everyone should save because of the Depression and not spend foolishly. We must have been trained right because it's very hard for me to spend money on a luxury even now.

I became a registered nurse after graduating from college in 1937. I worked until 1943, when I began raising three kids. After I got married the second time, I wasn't working anymore. So this insurance money was all the income I had for myself. My second husband was a veterinarian and he made good money, but you still like to have a little bit of mad money all for yourself.

I hide money everywhere. Once, I found a purse I hadn't used in ten years and I found a $20 bill in there. I get out my money in the cigar box and count it once in a while, just like a miser. The most I've ever had in there at one time is $600. And I'm not the only one. When my sister-in-law died in 1975, I went through her lingerie and found at least $400 in $100 bills tucked into her things!

So why do women do this? I think men would like to be in control of everything if they could. But they know they have to back down. Money doesn't bother me: If I need money, I just say to my husband, "I need $20 or

$40." My sister once said to me: "Why do you have to ask your husband for any money?"

LEARN TO SAVE RELIGIOUSLY

She's right. I think it's important for women to have a nest egg of their own. Even if they're only putting away $5 a month, even if they don't get married, they need to have money to fall back on. My daughter was able to make a down payment on a new home because she saved money. I have another daughter who doesn't save a cent. You can teach them all the same thing but then they go their own way.

These days, I handle the money in our marriage. I put everything on the computer, and I pay all the bills. Every once in a while I'll tell him what the balance is in the checkbook. I'm eighty-three and he's seventy-eight, so we're Social Security age. Money has not been a big issue for us.

I have a lot of friends who don't tell their husbands a lot of things about money. But if I was giving advice, I wouldn't tell women to keep money under a mattress or in a Jesus box. Young people should start saving money so they'll have something later on. They should start putting money into CDs, and growing their money for the future. Most young people I know don't even have health insurance. They're not taught about this in school. I live in Ferndale, a little town of about 1,400 people, and I see high school students with $20 bills buying cold drinks. They could be putting some of that away!

It's very important for women to have money of their own put away. It makes you feel good. It makes you feel important. If I want to go uptown and buy something, I can just go and do it. I don't have to beg my husband and say, "I want this, or I want that." I just go out and buy it. Even a sweatshirt, if I want it!

PENNIES FROM HEAVEN

My husband wanted to buy me a computer, for example, but I wanted something more than just a little computer. I bought a really good one with half of the money coming from the Jesus box. I just took out the money I needed, and I don't think he even knew how much that was!

It's all about security. I'm on a prayer chain on the computer, and I can't believe the troubles that some people have. So many broken marriages and sickness. People out of work. Sometimes I want to go on the computer and just pray for everybody.

Life Lessons from Maxine

1. It's important to start putting money away early in life, even if it's only $5 a week. But don't just stuff it in the mattress; women need to grow their money for the future, with CDs and other investments.

2. What a man doesn't know about your money won't hurt him, and it will probably help in the long run. You can do things *for* your family, with your money . . . and without his help.

3. Try to be conservative and save so you can do what you want. It's a little nicer if you have something secret. Just a little hiding place! Once in a while I'll send a friend who is a missionary in Africa a little bit! And there is no discussing it with anyone. No arguments with a man about this. I just do what I want to. And that feels good.

Catherine:	72 years old
Marital status:	Married since 1945; 4 children, 2 grandchildren
Job:	Homemaker
Home:	Des Moines, Iowa
$$ Strategy:	Secret account with her eldest daughter

"It's just a matter of being independent. . . .
He's always told me that if I want something,
I should go ahead and get it. But, like many women,
I don't want to have to have his permission."

I have an extremely generous husband. But his contention every time I brought up having my own checking account was: "You don't have to have your own checking account! Go out and get whatever you want!" "That is not the idea," I would tell him.

I love catalogs; I order junky stuff that he would question and argue with me about if I had to go to him for it. I don't want to have to hear him say: "What the heck is this from the Miles Kimball Cat Company? This is dumb stuff, Kate!" I said that one of these days I was going to open up my own checking account. So I did.

I opened it seven years ago with my daughter, Rose, who lives here in town. If I die, she can take this money out. How do I get money to put in the checking account? There are all kinds of devious ways to do this. I do a lot of shopping for my daughter. She works. I put the purchases on our charge. Then she gives me the check to pay off the credit card bill and I put the check in my secret account instead of in John's and my account. You see, John never pays attention to the charge accounts. Whatever it is, he pays. But I do all the bills and balance our checkbook. He sees the canceled checks.

Another way is with a sister who lives out of town. She would send me checks to buy all the nieces and nephews birthday presents. I would buy the presents with our credit card and then deposit the check in my secret account. Or I'll organize a luncheon outing for a group of friends, eight or ten of us. They'll each give me a check for $25. I put the checks in my account. I pay the bill with one big check from our joint account. He never questions that! The balance in my secret account is usually around $1,000. It's not a fortune but it's enough to have fun with.

I always keep these checks I get in our desk drawer. If thirty days go by and he doesn't say anything, then I know it's safe to deposit them in my secret account.

WHAT HE DOESN'T KNOW WON'T HURT, BUT WILL COST HIM

I also knock down on the house money $20 here, $50 there. This way, if I want to buy something for the grandkids that he thinks is stupid, I don't have to argue with him. I can go out and freely buy Nintendo for my grand-

son. My husband will say, "He's got enough of that stuff!"
All of my girlfriends do this in one way or another. None
of us works. It's just a matter of trying to be independent.
And I have to admit, it's kind of fun to be able to be
sneaky! He's always told me that if I want something, I
should go ahead and get it. But like many women, I don't
want to have to ask his permission! If I want to buy dumb
stuff, like a Halloween witch for the front yard, I should
be able to without a discussion.

My kids are in on it. John was in the service when we
married. He was an engineer, making $27 every two
weeks. Once he started to work, our big dream in life was
to bring home $100 a week. I used to wonder, How are
we going to pay this month (bill wise)? My first child was
born nine months and twelve days after we were married.
Money was a prime concern.

Until I came up with this secret checking account
idea, all our money was together. As time went on, he did
well. Getting anything I wanted was no problem. I never
worked. I went to college for two years, then we got married. I had four children. I never held a job outside the
home. I've done a lot of volunteer work.

My three daughters are such independent kids. All of
them work. They started in high school and worked
through college. They have the most wonderful marriages. They absolutely amaze me.

I got fed up. I was talking about this to John for years,
having my own account, but he would have none of it. It
offended his pride. That's why I keep it secret now. It's not
because it's such a big amount of money, it's because it

would hurt his pride. Someday I dream I will get a wonderful check from someone and I will slip it into this account. Most of what I buy with the money goes to my grandson, Frank, like I bought him a Santa Claus with a winking eye. My grandson is six. He thinks I'm his age!

About ten years ago, John changed a lot of his stocks into my name. That gave me a much better feeling. There were times earlier in the marriage when I felt very insecure. Here I was with all these kids. If he walked out, I didn't have any skills.

So now I have my secret account and when my husband's birthday comes, I am planning a surprise party for him at an expensive restaurant. And guess what? I'm going to pick up the tab myself—from all the money I have pilfered over the year!

Life Lessons from Catherine

Be sure you declare your independence when you get married and you have your own bank account. If you have to do it secretly, then do it. I would just caution any woman who is going to be a stay-at-home mom with this thought: You are worth a certain amount of money every month. That money should go into your account to spend as you want.

Rose Gingold, aka "Rose Miller": Died age 82
Marital status: Divorced in 1966; 2 children
Job: Housewife, secretary

174

Home: New York City

$$ Strategy: Created a new identity for herself. Got a part-time job
under an assumed name and Social Security number
unbeknownst to her husband, who had left her.
Invested her secret earnings. Left her children over
$100,000 when she died.

*"I was absolutely astounded when I found out about 'Rose Miller.'
I thought highly of my mother for it. She was a much more
resourceful and courageous person than she certainly ever
gave herself credit for. She was at her best as an old lady."*
—*Alfred Gingold, son*

My father left in 1966 but their divorce was not finalized
until 1977. For a good part of that time he was just doing
anything he could to draw it out to make life difficult for
her. He made her pay lawyers to fight for every dollar that
was rightfully hers, even child support. What that created
in her was a lot of anxiety. She thought she'd be out of a
house and home. She would get these IRS notices every
quarter, final notices that read to her that they would
come in and peel up the carpets. My mother was terrified.

In addition she was restricted from earning more than
$7,500 because her lawyers were arguing that she would
jeopardize her settlement unless she did little or no work,
as she had done in the previous thirty years of their mar-
riage. With these restrictions on how much she could
earn, and the financial pressures mounting from my fa-
ther—after eleven years of fighting through this divorce,
she got only $52,500, not a lot to live on for the rest of
your life—she decided to create another persona, Rose

Miller. She got another Social Security number under the name Rose Miller and she held jobs and filed tax returns. She was just like that guy in *The Day of the Jackal!* She got a name, picked it out of some death register I assume; she had the maiden name of her mother and her father's name written on her new birth certificate. *Rose Miller!* She cooked it all up!

Of the tax returns I have, she made between $10,000 and $15,000 a year doing secretarial work. He did not know she was working! In the last years of his life, he was very curious about her financial situation. He kept asking me and my sister if we were giving her money. He was wondering why she wasn't starving. He wanted her to suffer.

Did they argue about money? Did they! My father was the original never-buy-retail guy. He was a first-generation immigrant. They met in the Bronx. All his life he was hungry. My mother wanted finer things, to live on the Upper East Side. She wanted culture. She was full of life. Their marriage was in trouble before there were any children.

When she died in 1995, I found more than seventy bankbooks, some of them spanning fifty years, starting in the late 1930s, before she was married. I see deposits for $200 or $300 here and there. I think she was spiriting money away from my dad where she could, like most housewives in those days who had no money of their own and whose husbands controlled the money with an iron fist. When she got kind of batty at the end of her life, she would open and close accounts as a hobby.

SECRET LIVES, SECRET STASH

When she died, I was astounded at how much money she had accumulated in her humble and determined way. When she was alive, she always had the "glass half empty" mentality. You had the feeling she couldn't afford Tropicana, only the generic orange juice! She would always tell us, "Security, security, security! Invest in triple-tax-free bonds, whatever is safe." But in reality, my broker said, she invested like a Republican. She bought blue-chip stocks like AT&T and held on to them forever. She never sold a stock. She left a healthy six figures at least! I have to take my hat off to her!

Did I know about the other Rose? I knew she was working, but I only knew vaguely about "Rose Miller." I never took it seriously. Mail never came to the house for Rose Miller. She confided this scheme to her friends, the Silvers. They were in on this. They let her establish her mailing address there. I had no idea that she had gone to all this trouble. If you are doing something like this, I guess you do it all the way. As for Rose Miller's taxes, my mother would always befriend some guy at H&R Block who then would come over to her house and do it privately.

I thought highly of her for all this. She was a much more resourceful and courageous person than she certainly ever gave herself credit for. She was a crazy, very high-strung, very nervous person. She would really have benefited from feminism. She had all the instincts and all the frustrations!

She was better as an old lady than at any other time. A lot of her responsibilities were over. I came out thinking of her more highly. She was quite a gal.

Judy: 70 years old
Marital status: Married 48 years; 3 children, 4 grandchildren
Job: University professor
Home: Newport, California
$$ Strategy: Earns money that she puts in one of two joint
                accounts not monitored by her husband. She is free
                to spend as she pleases.

*"Earning your own money makes you feel powerful;
it's a state of mind where you feel that you can do anything
you damn please! I can write a check to a political candidate
that my husband might feel is excessive. I can spend $350
on a pair of earrings or have a massage when I want one.
I have the freedom to do crazy things that I could never
justify doing when I was 'just a housewife,' like flying first class,
spending $1,500 on a suit, or buying a Cadillac Seville
when a Ford would do."*

It wasn't always this way for me. I grew up poor on the east side of Los Angeles. I didn't even have a bicycle. I was a corporate wife for twenty years, didn't earn anything until I was forty-five years old. I got my Ph.D. when I was fifty. An article I wrote in *Harvard Business Week* titled "Ways Women Lead," plus two books written when I was sixty-one and sixty-five catapulted me onto the lecture circuit in addition to my teaching. I got big bucks for talking. (My husband said he'd pay me to stop talking!) Since I now was bringing home the bacon, I began to write big checks to women political candidates, and to causes I supported. I bought stock in a company because one of my students worked there, even though I knew nothing about the company. *I didn't feel guilty* because I had earned the money. Most women of my generation who married young and didn't work usually got an allowance from their husbands. I have to admit I didn't, but I always felt I had to be careful because I was not the breadwinner. I don't feel that way anymore. I am a breadwinner and I spend like crazy!

Luckily, I married a secure man and we have a trusting relationship when it comes to money. He knows I make money, and he loves it. But he never asks me how much I spend or where I spend it. He'd freak out if he knew of some of my expenditures! A man has to be very secure not to ask how much money his wife spends or how she spends it. I realize that most women have not been as lucky as I've been when it comes to money.

Judy's Life Lessons

1. Earning money feels good and it's never too late to start.
2. Ask for money when you provide a service—volunteering is nice, but getting paid is better.
3. Spend your money while you're healthy and able to enjoy it. Rainy days may never come.
4. Money doesn't matter unless you don't have any.

General Financial Tips for Your Sixties, Seventies, and Eighties

- Be sure your will is up to date and reflects how you want your assets and personal belongings distributed.
- Review your medical coverage.
- Consider working part-time if you can.
- Update your estate plan.
- Invest prudently—be careful not to put your nest egg in anything too risky.
- Find yourself an old, rich man. Then, as Joan Rivers advises: "Bring him to Las Vegas. Get married in one of those quickie chapels. And then, when he is playing blackjack, sneak up behind him and yell 'Boo!' Collect!"

179

6

Out of the Mattre$$ and into the Market

Accountants and Planners and Stocks, Oh My!

"I just hope I can do half as well with my future as you did with yours."

NOW *that you have squirreled away well and* have a nest egg to call your own, it's time to come out of the closet—the shoe box, the mattress, wherever it is you have been stashing your cash.

Because if I have heard this message once, I've heard it a hundred times from women in the know: If you are young or middle-aged, your money is losing money if it is not properly invested. Or, you might as well roll down the window and just throw your money away when you keep it in a savings account, since that is, in effect, what you are doing.

Clueless and Fearful

I know from my own experience how intimidating this world of money and investing can be. I have been financially fearful and clueless for most of my adult years, putting any savings we had in the bank. If I got daring, I put all of our money into CDs—certificates of deposit—for 5 or 6 percent interest for a year. Now I've learned that some money in a CD is fine. But too much is not too swift.

My husband is a swell guy and lets me handle his

money and mine, so at least I'm not fighting with him about control. (We, of course, argue about other things.) But since he has entrusted me with the job of doing the right thing with our money—making it grow, planning for our future—I have been too scared to do much with it but let it sit in the bank. Watching the stock market make gobs of money for everyone but us, I—and millions of women like me—could kick myself for not getting smarter and braver sooner.

Numerous studies show that most women are, in fact, timid about money. Facts and figures compiled by public television's "Nightly Business Report" found that:

- Women tend to put their money in low-interest bank accounts—they avoid the risk of losing money in the stock market for the sure thing of losing ground to inflation.
- Women earning six-figure salaries are no better prepared to deal with financial issues than women earning as little as $10,000 a year.
- Women save, on average, about half of what men save.
- Many men enjoy bragging about investment successes with their buddies; many women think it's inappropriate and unfeminine to discuss money.

According to "Nightly Business Report"'s longtime coanchor Cassie Seifert, 90 percent of women will be responsible for securing their families' financial futures at some point during their lives. Yet only 15 percent of married women, in a recent study by OppenheimerFunds, were getting experience in financial planning by making investment decisions for their households. Women of the baby-boom generation are, ironically, making great strides in the workforce, but most aren't building personal wealth.

So what's the deal with women when it comes to money? I've asked myself the same question. Why am I so timid? After all, when it comes to anything else, I get out there and make things happen. I even enjoy taking bold risks from time to time. Once I bet $1,000 on the Atlanta Falcons football team because a sports columnist at the newspaper where I worked wrote that they were strongly favored to win. While my husband was half asleep next to me, I wired the money by telephone to my longtime friend Russell, who was living in Las Vegas, and he, shocked and stunned at my request, placed the bet for me. I won, but I couldn't have even told you the name of the starting quarterback. Clearly, these risky larks are no way to handle your money. There are safer and surer things you can do with it. But where do you get the knowledge, comfort level, and motivation to do the right thing?

There's No Time Like the Present to Learn, So Dip into Your Piggy Bank and Buy a Clue

By starting to get educated about money and investing, I began to see the light and, hopefully, you will, too. It turns out money is not a dry, boring, or difficult subject. Just the opposite. Money can be fun. And you can meet a lot of terrific women—and men—in the process of learning about investing and actually doing it. Small investment clubs—like book clubs—are sprouting up all over the place and women are finding they are excellent at studying companies and making savvy choices in picking what stocks will do well in the years to come.

The turning point for me came a year ago when I attended an American Express seminar for women. Geri Zolna, a certified financial planner, told the audience of about fifty women one of those stories that just makes a lasting impression and inspires you to make changes in your life.

This was the story she told:

"A couple of years ago I treated myself to something. I decided to go to a health spa near San Diego—a real mind, body, soul place. I took a class called 'Inner Journey,' which was a meditation and relaxation thing. One day the instructor said something that really stuck with me. And what she said was, 'How you do anything is how you do everything.' I let it resonate for a while, but it made me think about what I did for a living."

"How you do anything is how you do everything." Right, I thought. Except for money. Many women are juggling many things at once and do it so well. Home, family, friends, careers, vacations. They are real go-getters, superbly organized, accomplished doers. Except when it comes to money. This was certainly true of me, I thought.

"There is a big gap in the way that women handle finances, compared to the way they handle everything else," says Zolna, who helps women become informed about investing and set on the road to financial fitness. So, the challenge becomes, how do I make myself as capable and confident as I am with all other things and apply it, without fear, to money and my financial security?

Getting Comfy with Cash—Your Financial Well-Being Depends on It! Want a Life? Get a Plan

All of the experts, including Zolna, agree on this: When you are thinking about your financial future you *must* write down your goals, dreams, and motivations. When we put something on paper, it becomes real.

This chapter will help you with some of the things you need to know for your financial well-being as women—beginning with writing down your goals and dreams and also including investment strategies to make these plans come true. You wouldn't be able to accomplish losing thirty pounds, for example, by just saying you were going on a diet. You would have a plan: No desserts. Or no fats. Or half-size portions. Otherwise it won't happen. Same thing with money.

Armed with this wisdom, I've made some dramatic changes in my own life. Since I started writing this book, I've opened my own account. I told my husband that I was going to do it. And it was surprising to very independent me how queasy I felt at first about doing this, as if I were keeping something from him. But once I did it, I have to say it has felt great, emancipating even. And that was the money—my very own money—that gave me the boost I needed to get my cash out of the mattress and into the stock market. I also hired a financial planner.

Why? Because most women, including myself, have had no financial education.

 So, as financial planner Ann B. Diamond asks, "How can you expect to feel comfortable with a topic that you've never been taught?"

She's right. Seek out a reputable certified financial planner, just like you would seek out a certified public accountant to help you with your taxes, or a decorator to help furnish your home. For a few hundred dollars—or if you buy a few helpful books for less than $50—you are on your way! And believe me—if I could do it, so could you. So here are some expert words from the experts:

A Conversation with Ann B. Diamond

Diamond is a financial counselor and author of Fear of Finance— The Women's Money Workbook for Achieving Financial Self-Confidence.

Q: You talk about stumbling blocks women have—fear of money, of investing, of losing what they have. What is your practical advice to women who have the extra barrier of a husband who insists on control of the money?

A: Control is a very complicated issue and touches on many parts of people's marriages. It's very deep-seated. It's not really about the money, it's about controlling the relationship and the other person. Some of that is better addressed by a therapist than a financial counselor. That being said, however, I think that women can start to do small things that begin to shift the balance of power a little bit.

STEP ONE: HAVE YOUR OWN CREDIT CARDS. You need credit cards for protection purposes whether or not you earn money on your own.

If you're married and not working outside the home, you can still be the primary holder of at least one of the credit cards that you and your husband possess. It's the primary holder who would keep the card in the case of divorce or death. If you apply for your own card and are told you need a cosigner, ask someone other than your husband so that the record you are establishing is yours and not his. If you had credit cards before you were married, keep your individual cards and you will maintain your own history.

Here is a horrible example of what can happen if you are not the primary holder of at least one credit card. If there is an emergency, you are sunk. Example: A woman was traveling with her husband when he died in an accident. All their credit cards were in both of their names, but she was not the primary holder of any of them. When she tried to use the cards for emergency airfare and to make arrangements, she could not use any of them. Money had to be sent to her.

STEP TWO: OPEN YOUR OWN CHECKING OR SAVINGS ACCOUNTS. If you work, you should contribute to the household on a pro rata basis in a joint account, and then have some of your own money in your own separate account so you don't have to have a discussion with your husband about everything you want to buy for yourself, for your kids, or for him. Having your own checking account really relieves a lot of the day-to-day discussions, arguments, and tensions over every bill that comes through your hands.

190

STEP THREE: USE HUMOR AND BE CREATIVE ABOUT THE SMALL STUFF! My husband would get very upset when he would see me on the telephone for a long time. Tired of him carping about this, I said to him one day: "You know what? From now on the telephone is free! You will never see another phone bill!" And for the past fifteen years, I have had the bill come to my office instead of our home and he never sees it.

We have never had another discussion about the phone. It works! Using humor is a great way to resolve a lot of these insignificant, petty annoyances that can cause a blowup! If you make it light and do it the way I did with the telephone bill, it can really solve the problem.

Another thing I do is to buy something at the supermarket to cook for dinner and take off the price tag. We prefer to eat at home because the meals are more delicious and cost a fraction of the price of a restaurant meal. Therefore I am not concerned when I buy ingredients in the market that are really expensive, like the veal scallopini I bought the other night. It's about $20 a pound. I take the price tag off! He cooks! When he sees the price tag off, he laughs! He'll say: "Did you have to take out a second mortgage on the apartment for this?"

I know what my husband's hot buttons are, so by using humor and these little games, we get along just fine. Oftentimes in a marriage, people like to stick the dagger in the other person. When you know someone's hot buttons, there are little ways to get at them. You can plant little seeds. To me, there is no purpose in that. Like I said, I want peace in my home.

191

If you buy yourself an outfit and you don't want to have an argument, there is no need to model it that night! Wait a few weeks. So when he asks, "Where did you get that outfit?," you can say, "Oh, it's been in my closet. I just haven't worn it in a while."

I also feel that for homemakers—especially for women who worked before they had children, and the couple made a conscious decision that the wife would stay home to raise their children—there really should be a payment system. Raising children is a JOB! And a very important one! It costs a lot of money to have someone stay home with your kids if you work. There should be a discussion of how much a wife gets paid for that job and it should be her money to do with as she pleases. It also makes for a better marriage; it makes the husband more appreciative of what his wife does and cuts down on a lot of the arguing.

It's all about communicating. What I would tell women to say to their husbands is this: If I died, what would a housekeeper cost you? What would a nanny cost you? How much is that worth? You'd pay someone else. Why is it less valuable if your wife does it? Unfortunately, a lot of women buy into men's thinking that it's their job to do it and they should not be paid. This is why a lot of women don't have life insurance. They don't think that what they do has value.

So treat your marriage as if you are starting a business.

Try to have a year's worth of expenses behind you before you leave your job to raise kids. Start putting money away before you get pregnant.

Q: What do you suggest to women whose husbands have total control of the family purse strings and who keep their wives in the dark?

A: Men like this, although they give lip service to being the family protector and provider, are not protecting their families. Just the opposite. What happens to the wife and children if something unexpected happens to the husband? Say he drowns on his boat? His wife would not know where things were or what to do! That would be a disaster, and it happens all too often. If women sat down and said to their husbands: "*Look,* one of the things about a marriage is that we try to make each other feel comfortable. I feel a lot of anxiety about not knowing anything about our finances. If something happened to you, I don't even know where the bank accounts are. It makes me petrified and I want to know. I need to know." Most men would say okay!

Q: Some women don't want to know about the family finances. They think it is beyond them or that it's boring.

A: This is true and it is a bad decision to keep your head in the sand about your financial matters. I had a client who used to have drills for his wife! He'd come home and say to her, "*I died today.* What are you going to do?" She said, "Cry!" He would say, "No, that's not the right answer!" And he would do this until she got it. The right answer he kept drilling into her was "Call our lawyer, insurance agent, broker, and accountant! That's what you should do. And know their phone numbers and where all your important papers are." She said it was so painful. But she learned so she could stop thinking about it with anxiety. The woman later told me: "It did happen and I knew exactly what to do!"

Humor makes money a lot easier to deal with. A lot of this is about dealing with our mortality.

Q: What can women do who have to keep their money hidden from their husbands and yet want to legally invest it somewhere?

A: Buy E-bonds (government-issued savings bonds). You won't earn very much (4.5 percent interest) but it's better than nothing and you don't pay taxes on it until it matures or until you redeem it. The income doesn't show up on any forms. You can put them in your vault. They don't show up on your tax returns year by year, until they are redeemed.

It's always best, however, if you can be open with your mate. Conceptually I don't like being deceptive. What you are doing is covering up a bigger problem. It makes better sense to deal with the underlying cause. But I understand that not everyone is in a marriage where they can have input into the money decisions.

Q: What are the biggest changes you've seen between the sexes over money?

A: The biggest change I've seen over the years is that I used to get women who came in after their divorce and talked about how they were treated unfairly in the proceedings. Now I have women coming in *before* the divorce, saying things like: "I know he sold his business. But where is the money? It doesn't show up anywhere! He thinks I'm a complete idiot and I'm not. *Where is his money?*" I always tell women the first place to look is the tax return! If it shows income that is not in line with what you know to be the truth, start demanding, *"Show me the money!"* Mostly though, this is a rich person's problem.

Q: What is the biggest mistake women make when they squirrel away money?

A: They don't realize the *power of compounding.* I always tell young people: If you put $2,000 in an IRA for five years, that's $10,000. If you are in your twenties, and never put another penny in, by the time you retire, forty years later, with 10 percent compounding, that $10,000 will become over $450,000. WOW!

Q: How do you suggest couples set up their finances? Together or apart?

A: Every couple has to find their own way—what works for them. It seems to me that people who have the least amount of conflict each have their own checking account and a joint checking account for household expenses. Each person contributes to the household expenses on a pro rata basis—meaning you each contribute a certain amount depending on what you earn.

A lot of couples decide who is paying for what. I pay the phone bill, my husband pays the electric bill. Why? I have no idea. In my house, I pay for the goodies—the vacations, the gifts. We sort of split the household expenses.

He pays for all his personal stuff and the car. Some couples find it works by pooling all their money and paying the bills from the one pot of money. It's whatever works for you.

We are very married after twenty-one years; we understand each other. For people who are just starting out and have had their own accounts and are now merging, it's best to establish a discipline. This is what I'll contribute, this is what you'll contribute.

Q: Your biggest piece of advice for everyone?

A: Set goals! Long-term, medium-term, and shorter-term goals of what you want to have, how you want to live. A wife can get very resentful if her husband is buying a lot of stereo equipment when she is trying to put away money for the kids' education, to buy a larger apartment, or to go on a much-needed vacation. That's why I emphasize the goals so much. Figure out what yours are and what your husband's are . . . together and apart. The key is communication—and money. Without money, you can't have your dreams together, you can't leave if that's what you need to do, you can't do anything. That is what keeps so many women in bad marriages.

Also, you must be religious about allocating money toward your goals from every paycheck, not just when you have extra (which will be seldom, if ever). Aim to dedicate 10 percent of your gross income toward financing your objective. In other words, if you earn $20,000 a year, $2,000 is the magic number to save. If that is not possible now, save 3 percent of $20,000, or $600. Saving

How to Hide Money from Your Husband . . .

$600 per year is $50 a month, or $25 per paycheck if you are paid twice a month. Whenever you get a raise, increase the funding by 1 percent, so if you get a raise to $22,250, you would put away 4 percent of $22,250 or $900 per year, $75 per month or $37.50 per paycheck.

Pay Yourself First! The First Check You Write Every Month Should Be to You!

Perhaps the single most important lesson of saving and investing is this: Take care of *your* needs first. That was the message of a recent conversation I had with Cassie Seifert, the former coanchor of public television's "Nightly Business Report" and producer of "Women and Money," a ninety-minute video. It's not enough to know the ins and outs of investing; you need to get your priorities straight. And Seifert makes no bones about what they are:

"One of the things that a lot of women tend to do is to wait until they have paid the rest of the bills before they put a little money aside for themselves," says Seifert. "Women need to change their priorities—whether it's for their open savings account that they tell their husband about or for their secret little fund. They really need to pay themselves first, and that should be the first money that's set aside, because that's the money that's going to be really important to them in the long term.

"When you sit down to pay the bills, give yourself a talk. And before you write any checks, think about what's really important to you; think about your goals and your dreams. When you ask yourself, what are my dreams, what do I want to do, what will be fulfilling to me in my life—most of those things require money. If women could just get themselves to focus on the big, important things they really want—whether it's fine furnishings or to educate their grandchildren or to travel—they can start to save for those dreams and make them a reality.

"When I handed out surveys at a recent 'Women and Money' seminar, I was surprised by how many women said they wanted to travel, wanted second homes, wanted to pay for their children's or their grandchildren's education. These were real priorities for them. If women can get themselves to think in terms of, if not their goals, at least their dreams, and what's important long term, I think that will encourage them to put their money away. Or as some people say, they'll pay themselves before they pay the phone bill or gas company."

But isn't that the whole psychological issue with women—that they can't put their needs first?

"My point is, if women don't put themselves first, they can be hurting their children, their families, in the long term. Women who end up alone, as so many women do later in life, and who haven't 'paid themselves first' or haven't taken care of themselves financially end up being a burden on their children. And women are so giving, they'll clean out their secret bank account to make their children's tuition payments. Or they will lend money or give money to their children to make a down payment on

198

their first home, not thinking that if they don't have a plan in place to build money to support themselves later in life, they're going to be a burden on their children. And it happens over and over again. Ask young people: Would they prefer that mom make a down payment now on their house and come to live with them in a few years because she's got no money in the bank to live on herself? Or would they prefer to make their down payment themselves, and know that their mom is secure and independent in a few years? Most would choose the latter."

But isn't it hard to convince young people in their twenties and thirties who marry that the best time to save for the future is now? They think the future is so far away, that planning for retirement is something you do in your fifties or sixties.

"That's true," Seifert says. "Some women live on the edge, particularly single moms. They say, 'I can't possibly invest.' But there are a bunch of mutual funds where money managers will be happy to help you, even if you invest $25 to $50 a month. You just have to make the commitment to do it. Managers can invest in a mix of funds for you. And as long as you are willing to do it— $25 to $50 dollars a month—almost everybody, including people who are really living on the edge, can come up with an extra $25 or $50. (That's just $6.50 or $12.50 a week!) And you know, the earlier you start, the better off you are long term. It doesn't have to be a large amount of money. Any little bit helps, and even if you start off small, there are rewards. There are emotional rewards. Even if you put away $25 a month for a few months, you'll say:

'Gosh, I have a couple of hundred dollars saved, and I made a little money on my couple of hundred dollars. I can really do this. Maybe I can put away $30 a month now, because it's rewarding. It's fun.' "

Conclusion:
The Ten Commandments of Money
and Marriage

Life *changes. In the three years since I first* started researching this book, many of the women with the darkest stories now have happy ones to tell. And, sadly, a few of the happy marriages are struggling.

Meryl, for example, the Chicago public relations executive whose husband traded her in after twenty-five years of marriage for a newer, blonder version, fell in love and is getting remarried this year. Her anger and bitterness are behind her. But she learned her lessons well and will make sure that what money and property she brings to her second marriage will remain legally hers and her children's. What Meryl and her new husband create after they say "I do" will be theirs together.

Veronica, the young hair colorist who hid her nest egg in the freezer to save for her and her husband's dreams, will still see them come true some day, but perhaps not with Tony. The rift has nothing to do with money. It's an overbearing, meddling mother-in-law who is making the marriage intolerable.

All this goes to show that you never know. But the one thing that you can always bet on is that having a nest egg, money of your own, is a key to survival—in or out of marriage. As long as you are alive, money is a necessity for you to move forward in life and be a strong, independent, and free person.

Women are now employed in record numbers, 63 million strong, and they represent 46 percent of America's workforce. They also own one third, or 8 million, of the nation's businesses. This is real power, but we need to make sure that some of that money is being set aside in a nest egg marked "HERS."

Most of us are going to live even longer, healthier lives and we simply must plan for the future. Demographers project that half of all the girls born today will live past 100. So you or your daughter, if you have one, better start feathering that nest in a hurry. Living well is not getting any cheaper, although your aging husband probably will. And since chances are that you are going to outlive him, you'd better outsave him, too.

The Ten Commandments of Money and Marriage

1. Don't marry or live with a man who wants to control the money—or you.
2. The women who get hurt the most are those who have had no interest in their finances.
3. Don't feel guilty about starting your nest egg! Just feel guilty you didn't start it sooner.
4. The wallet is the window into the soul of marriage.
5. Hide money from your husband for your husband.
6. Don't ever surrender the financial reins to your husband. Hold on to both of them; share the reins with him, but never let go of them completely.
7. The first check you write each month when you pay the bills should be to you. Pay yourself first!
8. Stand up to your husband and say, "This is what has to be!"
9. Nice husbands do not exempt you from having a nest egg. Squirrel away even more since it will be for the two of you.
10. A little money stashed away always puts a smile on a woman's face.

Appendix

Form **4506**	**Request for Copy or Transcript of Tax Form**	OMB No. 1545-0429
(Rev. May 1997) Department of the Treasury Internal Revenue Service	► Read instructions before completing this form. ► Type or print clearly. Request may be rejected if the form is incomplete or illegible.	

Note: *Do not use this form to get tax account information. Instead, see instructions below.*

1a Name shown on tax form. If a joint return, enter the name shown first.	1b First social security number on tax form or employer identification number (see instructions)
2a If a joint return, spouse's name shown on tax form	2b Second social security number on tax form

3 Current name, address (including apt., room, or suite no.), city, state, and ZIP code

4 Address, (including apt., room, or suite no.), city, state, and ZIP code shown on the last return filed if different from line 3

5 If copy of form or a tax return transcript is to be mailed to someone else, enter the third party's name and address

6 If we cannot find a record of your tax form and you want the payment refunded to the third party, check here . . . . . ► ☐

7 If name in third party's records differs from line 1a above, enter that name here (see instructions) ►

8 Check only one box to show what you want. There is **no charge** for items 8a, b, and c:
 a ☐ Tax return transcript of Form 1040 series filed during the **current calendar year** and the **3 prior calendar years** (see instructions).
 b ☐ Verification of nonfiling.
 c ☐ Form(s) W-2 information (see instructions).
 d ☐ Copy of tax form and all attachments (including Form(s) W-2, schedules, or other forms). **The charge is $23 for each period requested.**
   Note: *If these copies must be certified for court or administrative proceedings, see instructions and check here* . . . . ► ☐

9 If this request is to meet a requirement of one of the following, check all boxes that apply.
   ☐ Small Business Administration   ☐ Department of Education   ☐ Department of Veterans Affairs   ☐ Financial institution

10 **Tax form number** (Form 1040, 1040A, 941, etc.)

11 **Tax period(s)** (year or period ended date). If more than four, see instructions.

12 Complete only if **line 8d** is checked. Amount due:
 a Cost for each period . . . . . . $ 23.00
 b Number of tax periods requested on line 11
 c Total cost. Multiply line 12a by line 12b. $
 Full payment must accompany your request. Make check or money order payable to "Internal Revenue Service."

Caution: *Before signing, make sure all items are complete and the form is dated.*

I declare that I am either the taxpayer whose name is shown on line 1a or 2a, or a person authorized to obtain the tax information requested. I am aware that based upon this form, the IRS will release the tax information requested to any party shown on line 5. The IRS has no control over what that party does with the information.

Please Sign Here

Signature. See instructions. If other than taxpayer, attach authorization document.   Date

Title (if line 1a above is a corporation, partnership, estate, or trust)

Spouse's signature   Date

Telephone number of requester ( )
Best time to call

TRY A TAX RETURN TRANSCRIPT (see line 8a instructions)

Instructions

Section references are to the Internal Revenue Code.

TIP: If you had your tax form filled in by a paid preparer, check first to see if you can get a copy from the preparer. This may save you both time and money.

Purpose of Form.—Use Form 4506 to get a tax return transcript, verification that you did not file a Federal tax return, Form W-2 information, or a copy of a tax form. Allow 6 weeks after you file a tax form before you request a copy of it or a transcript. For W-2

information, wait 13 months after the end of the year in which the wages were earned. For example, wait until Feb. 1999 to request W-2 information for wages earned in 1997.

Do not use this form to request Forms 1099 or tax account information. See this page for details on how to get these items.

Note: *Form 4506 must be received by the IRS within 60 calendar days after the date you signed and dated the request.*

How Long Will It Take?—You can get a tax return transcript or verification of nonfiling within 7 to 10 workdays after the IRS receives your request. It can take up to 60 calendar

days to get a copy of a tax form or W-2 information. To avoid any delay, be sure to furnish all the information asked for on Form 4506.

Forms 1099.—If you need a copy of a Form 1099, contact the payer. If the payer cannot help you, call or visit the IRS to get Form 1099 information.

Tax Account Information.—If you need a statement of your tax account showing any later changes that you or the IRS made to the original return, request tax account information. Tax account information lists

(Continued on back)

For Privacy Act and Paperwork Reduction Act Notice, see back of form.   Cat. No. 41721E   Form **4506** (Rev. 5-97)

Appendix

certain items from your return, including any later changes.

To request tax account information, write or visit an IRS office or call the IRS at the number listed in your telephone directory.

If you want your tax account information sent to a third party, complete **Form 8821**, Tax Information Authorization. You may get this form by phone (call 1-800-829-3676) or on the Internet (at http://www.irs.ustreas.gov).

Line 1b.—Enter your employer identification number (EIN) **only** if you are requesting a copy of a **business** tax form. Otherwise, enter the first social security number (SSN) shown on the tax form.

Line 2b.—If requesting a copy or transcript of a joint tax form, enter the second SSN shown on the tax form.

Note: If you do not complete line 1b and, if applicable, line 2b, there may be a delay in processing your request.

Line 5.—If you want someone else to receive the tax form or tax return transcript (such as a CPA, an enrolled agent, a scholarship board, or a mortgage lender), enter the name and address of the individual. If we cannot find a record of your tax form, we will notify the third party directly that we cannot fill the request.

Line 7.—Enter the name of the client, student, or applicant if it is different from the name shown on line 1a. For example, the name on line 1a may be the parent of a student applying for financial aid. In this case, you would enter the student's name on line 7 so the scholarship board can associate the tax form or tax return transcript with their file.

Line 8a.—If you want a tax return transcript, check this box. Also, on line 10 enter the tax form number and on line 11 enter the tax period for which you want the transcript.

A tax return transcript is available only for returns in the 1040 series (Form 1040, Form 1040A, 1040EZ, etc.). It shows most line items from the original return, including accompanying forms and schedules. In many cases, a transcript will meet the requirement of any lending institution such as a financial institution, the Department of Education, or the Small Business Administration. It may also be used to verify that you did not claim any itemized deductions for a residence.

Note: A tax return transcript does not reflect any changes you or the IRS made to the original return. If you want a statement of your tax account with the changes, see **Tax Account Information** on page 1.

Line 8b.—Check this box only if you want proof from the IRS that you did not file a return for the year. Also, on line 11 enter the tax period for which you want verification of nonfiling.

Line 8c.—If you want only Form(s) W-2 information, check this box. Also, on line 10 enter "Form(s) W-2 only" and on line 11 enter the tax period for which you want the information.

You may receive a copy of your actual Form W-2 or a transcript of the information, depending on how your employer filed the form. However, state withholding information is not shown on a transcript. If you have filed your tax return for the year the wages were earned, you can get a copy of the actual Form W-2 by requesting a complete copy of your return and paying the required fee.

Contact your employer if you have lost your current year's Form W-2 or have not received it by the time you are ready to prepare your tax return.

Note: If you are requesting information about your spouse's Form W-2, your spouse must sign Form 4506.

Line 8d.—If you want a certified copy of a tax form for court or administrative proceedings, check the box to the right of line 8d. It will take at least 60 days to process your request.

Line 11.—Enter the year(s) of the tax form or tax return transcript you want. For fiscal-year filers or requests for quarterly tax forms, enter the date the period ended; for example, 3/31/96, 6/30/96, etc. If you need more than four different tax periods, use additional Forms 4506. Tax forms filed 6 or more years ago may not be available for making copies. However, tax account information is generally still available for these periods.

Line 12c.—Write your SSN or EIN and "Form 4506 Request" on your check or money order. If we cannot fill your request, we will refund your payment.

Signature.—Requests for copies of tax forms or tax return transcripts to be sent to a third party must be signed by the person whose name is shown on line 1a or by a person authorized to receive the requested information.

Copies of tax forms or tax return transcripts of a jointly filed return may be furnished to either the husband or the wife. Only one signature is required. However, see the line 8c instructions. Sign Form 4506 exactly as your name appeared on the original tax form. If you changed your name, **also** sign your current name.

For a corporation, the signature of the president of the corporation, or any principal officer and the secretary, or the principal officer and another officer are generally required. For more details on who may obtain tax information on corporations, partnerships, estates, and trusts, see section 6103.

If you are **not** the taxpayer shown on line 1a, you must attach your authorization to receive a copy of the requested tax form or tax return transcript. You may **attach a copy of the authorization document** if the original has already been filed with the IRS. This will generally be a **power of attorney** (Form 2848), or **other authorization**, such as Form 8821, or evidence of entitlement (for Title 11 Bankruptcy or Receivership Proceedings). If the taxpayer is deceased, you must send Letters Testamentary or other evidence to establish that you are authorized to act for the taxpayer's estate.

Where To File.—Mail Form 4506 with the correct total payment attached, if required, to the **Internal Revenue Service Center** for the place where you lived when the requested tax form was filed.

Note: You must use a separate form for each service center from which you are requesting a copy of your tax form or tax return transcript.

If you lived in:	Use this address:
New Jersey, New York (New York City and counties of Nassau, Rockland, Suffolk, and Westchester)	1040 Waverly Ave. Photocopy Unit Stop 532 Holtsville, NY 11742
New York (all other counties), Connecticut, Maine, Massachusetts, New Hampshire, Rhode Island, Vermont	310 Lowell St. Photocopy Unit Stop 679 Andover, MA 01810
Florida, Georgia, South Carolina	4800 Buford Hwy Photocopy Unit Stop 91 Doraville, GA 30362
Indiana, Kentucky, Michigan, Ohio, West Virginia	P.O. Box 145500 Photocopy Unit Stop 521 Cincinnati, OH 45250
Kansas, New Mexico, Oklahoma, Texas	3651 South Interregional Hwy Photocopy Unit Stop 6716 Austin, TX 73301
Alaska, Arizona, California (counties of Alpine, Amador, Butte, Calaveras, Colusa, Contra Costa, Del Norte, El Dorado, Glenn, Humboldt, Lake, Lassen, Marin, Mendocino, Modoc, Napa, Nevada, Placer, Plumas, Sacramento, San Joaquin, Shasta, Sierra, Siskiyou, Solano, Sonoma, Sutter, Tehama, Trinity, Yolo, and Yuba), Colorado, Idaho, Montana, Nebraska, Nevada, North Dakota, Oregon, South Dakota, Utah, Washington, Wyoming	P.O. Box 9941 Photocopy Unit Stop 6734 Ogden, UT 84409
California (all other counties), Hawaii	5045 E. Butler Avenue Photocopy Unit Stop 52180 Fresno, CA 93888
Illinois, Iowa, Minnesota, Missouri, Wisconsin	2306 E Bannister Road Photocopy Unit Stop 6700, Annex 1 Kansas City, MO 64999
Alabama, Arkansas, Louisiana, Mississippi, North Carolina, Tennessee	P.O. Box 30309 Photocopy Unit Stop 46 Memphis, TN 38130
Delaware, District of Columbia, Maryland, Pennsylvania, Virginia, a foreign country, or A.P.O. or F.P.O address	11601 Roosevelt Blvd. Photocopy Unit DP 536 Philadelphia, PA 19255

Privacy Act and Paperwork Reduction Act Notice.—We ask for the information on this form to establish your right to gain access to your tax form or transcript under the Internal Revenue Code, including sections 6103 and 6109. We need it to gain access to your tax form or transcript in our files and properly respond to your request. If you do not furnish the information, we will not be able to fill your request. We may give the information to the Department of Justice or other appropriate law enforcement official, as provided by law.

You are not required to provide the information requested on a form that is subject to the Paperwork Reduction Act unless the form displays a valid OMB control number. Books or records relating to a form or its instructions must be retained as long as their contents may become material in the administration of any Internal Revenue law. Generally, tax returns and return information are confidential, as required by section 6103.

The time needed to complete and file this form will vary depending on individual circumstances. The estimated average time is: **Recordkeeping,** 13 min.; **Learning about the law or the form,** 7 min.; **Preparing the form,** 26 min.; and **Copying, assembling, and sending the form to the IRS,** 17 min.

If you have comments concerning the accuracy of these time estimates or suggestions for making this form simpler, we would be happy to hear from you. You can write to the Tax Forms Committee, Western Area Distribution Center, Rancho Cordova, CA 95743-0001. **DO NOT** send the form to this address. Instead, see **Where To File** on this page

Equal Work, Unequal Paycheck

Computer Programmers

Men: $39,624
Women: $35,412

    - $4,212

Lawyers

Men: $60,892
Women: $49,816

    - $11,076

Secretaries*

Men: $22,932
Women: $20,540

    - $2,392

* secretaries / stenographers / typists

Source: National Committee on Pay Equity, 1996, using Bureau of Labor Statistics average annual earnings data.

Education and the Pay Gap

$20,044	$30,004	$31,096	$45,015
High-School-Educated Women	High-School-Educated Men	College-Educated Women	College-Educated Men

Source: U.S. Census, based on average annual earnings, white men and women, 1995.

Printed in the United States
By Bookmasters